pizza
calzone & focaccia

pizza
calzone & focaccia

Maxine Clark photography by Richard Jung

RYLAND
PETERS
& SMALL

LONDON NEW YORK

Dedication
For Julia and more happy times
in bella Napoli

Design and photographic art direction
  Steve Painter
Commissioning Editor Julia Charles
Editor Céline Hughes
Production Simon Walsh
Publishing Director Alison Starling

Food Stylist Maxine Clark
Assistant Food Stylists Lizzie Harris,
  Susie Plant and Jo Lee
Prop Stylist Róisín Nield

Indexer Hilary Bird

First published in the United Kingdom
in 2007
by Ryland Peters & Small
20–21 Jockey's Fields
London WC1R 4BW
www.rylandpeters.com

10 9 8 7 6 5 4 3 2 1

Text © Maxine Clark 2007
Design and photographs
© Ryland Peters & Small 2007

Photography by Richard Jung,
except page 9, by Martin Brigdale

ISBN 978 1 84597 372 8

A catalogue record for this book
is available from the British Library.

Printed and bound in China

Notes

• All spoon measurements are level unless
otherwise stated.

• Eggs are large unless otherwise specified.
Uncooked or partially cooked eggs should
not be served to the very old, frail, young
children, pregnant women or those with
compromised immune systems.

Author's Acknowledgements

My thanks go to editors Julia, Rachel and
Céline at RPS who all worked on the book;
art director and designer Steve for his keen
eye and keener taste buds; photographer
Richard Jung for his calmness while his
studio was dusted in a cloud of flour, and
for really beautiful emotive photographs.
Thanks to Róisín for once again finding
incredible atmospheric props and
backgrounds; Lizzie Harris, Susie Plant and
Jo Lee for help with mixing, kneading,
patting and shopping.

contents

introduction

I was bitten by the pizza bug in the best of all places, a huge farmhouse kitchen in Tuscany. I was working with chef Alvaro Maccioni teaching Italian cookery classes, when we discovered that a huge bread/pizza oven was hidden behind a small, blackened iron door. Aristide, the old man who swept and set the huge fires in the lodge, set and lit the oven, first with faggots of fine chestnut branches to quickly warm the porous base and domed brick roof, changing to metre-long, thinnish logs of seasoned broadleaf wood to sustain the heat and create a bed of wood coals over the base. After two to three hours it was ready. The live coals were swept to one side in a pile, the base or sole of the oven swept clean with a wet brush, and another log or two placed on top of the coals to maintain the heat.

During this time, we had mixed and energetically kneaded dough, shaped it into balls, and set them on a huge wooden tray, dusting the tops copiously with flour. The dough rose easily on that chilly October day, as the heat from the now roaring fire-pit of an oven was tremendous. The balls rose and cracked their floury caps. These were upturned and patted or rolled out, toppings added and in turn, guided by Alvaro or twinkly-eyed Aristide, everyone slipped their pizza onto the *pala* or peel and shot it into the oven. 5 minutes later we were munching on what was voted 'the best pizza in the world' and sipping ice cold beer.

Since then, I have fired up different sizes and types of ovens both at home and in Italy, and made countless pizzas, learning more with every dough made and every pizza patted. I have tried to make the recipes in this book home-oven friendly, as I am well aware that most people will not have a wood-fired oven to hand, or indeed the time needed to fire it up. Good pizza *can* be made at home, as long as the dough is soft and pillowy, the oven is hot, and there's a heavy baking sheet or bakestone inside. Although the taste of the wood smoke won't be there, the pizza will bake with a nice chewy crust. Most importantly, the ingredients must be the best and freshest, and there's no room for kitchen leftovers.

Pizza is said to have originated on the streets of Naples, to feed and fill ordinary working people cheaply. Its roots are distinctly southern Italian, and pizza is considered a food of the city. Pizza alla Napoletana is always 'open pizza' (never filled, folded and baked). However, the way to eat pizza in the street is to fold it in quarters, hold it in a napkin and munch it like a sandwich. The Associazione Vera Pizza Napoletana lays down strict rules for the making and cooking of pizza in order to be able to sell it as Pizza Napoletana. Little stuffed and deep-fried pizzelle and panzerotti are other examples of street food from Naples and Campania. In Rome, pizza is sold by the metre (or its parts). Throughout Italy, other types of flat hearth breads, such as focaccia and schiacciata, were traditionally made at home on the hot hearth where the embers had been.

The only ingredients necessary to make pizza dough are flour, salt, yeast and water. I like to add olive oil as it gives a good texture and flavour to the dough when baked at home. Salt will bring the flavour out of the dough and strengthen the crust but if you are using a flaky sea or crystal salt, make sure it is finely ground, or dissolve it in the warm water before adding it to the flour. Any type of yeast you are happy with will do – just follow the manufacturer's instructions, using the liquid specified in the recipe. As for water, the softer the water, the better the dough, so I would use filtered water or even bottled water in hard water areas. Other breads, like focaccia, rely on olive oil for flavour, so you must use extra virgin olive oil. It doesn't have to be an expensive one – a supermarket blend of extra virgin olive oils will do. Always anoint your piping hot pizza with extra virgin olive oil (flavoured or not) before you eat it. Not only will it look better, it will also taste sublime!

My final advice to any novice pizza-maker is to keep the choice of topping as simple as you can to truly appreciate the flavours. The crust is all-important and turns soggy if it is weighed down too much. Slice meat and vegetables thinly and don't smother the base with sauce or cheese. Most important of all, eat it hot, hot, hot, straight out of the oven. I hope you enjoy using this book – I cooked every one of the pizzas for the photographs, and we never tired of eating them at the studio as they were all so different from each other that there was always something new to taste. Go on, get your hands in some dough right now and bake a fragrant pizza. You don't need any special ingredients – just start off with an olive oil, salt and garlic topping and savour your first real pizza.

basics

equipment and utensils

Making pizza dough couldn't be easier, and when you become familiar with the process, you can guess the quantities by eye. To make really good pizza, you will need a few basic items in the kitchen, the most important being your hands!

You should have a good selection of the usual suspects: **mixing bowls**, **measuring spoons**, **measuring jugs**, **weighing scales** or **cup measures**; a good **sharp knife** or **pastry wheel** for cutting dough; a **large serrated knife** for cutting focaccia.

My favourite gadget is a **pastry scraper** which can be used as a knife, scoop and board scraper or cleaner. Scrapers come in all guises but they usually comprise a rectangular metal 'blade', one edge of which is covered by a wooden or plastic handle that fits into the palm of your hand.

If you are really serious about pizza-making and want to make dough in quantity, an **electric food mixer** will take the pain out of mixing and kneading large batches of dough, although there's nothing quite as satisfying as hand-kneading a big, soft pillow of dough.

Clingfilm is the modern alternative to a damp tea towel. This is used to cover a dough when it is rising to keep it moist and to stop the surface drying out and forming a crust, which can impair the rising.

Clingfilm on its own will stick to a dough, so either lightly rub the dough with a little olive oil, or spray or brush the clingfilm lightly with oil before covering the dough. Alternatively, you can cover the rising dough with a large, upturned mixing bowl.

Non-stick baking parchment is a revelation for making pizza. There is no need to dust the bottom of the pizza with masses of extra flour (which never cooks) to prevent it sticking. Dusting with cornmeal is in no way authentic and it sticks to the dough, ruining the texture.

A good, steady work surface at the right height is essential for energetic kneading. The surface should be able to cope with sticky dough, flour and olive oil and should be easy to clean.

A **flour sifter** or **shaker** is useful as it will limit the flour you sprinkle onto the dough and is always to hand. Alternatively, you can make do with a little bowl of extra flour on the side, for dusting.

An **olive-oil pourer** will allow you to drizzle small amounts of olive oil onto a pizza or into a dough. Some are cans with long spouts, and some neatly fit into the olive-oil bottle itself.

A **water spray** mists a dough with just enough water to keep it moist.

Pastry brushes are always handy in a kitchen, especially when brushing the tops of calzone with oil or water and for brushing the edges of dough with water before sealing.

Biscuit cutters will cut dough into smaller shapes for stuffing or filling.

You will need one or two **deep, heavy metal tins/pizza pans/springform cake tins** for deep-pan pizzas and focaccias; **heavy rectangular tins** and **baking trays** for larger pizzas; and good, heavy, rimless **baking sheets** (or turn them upside down) for baking pizzas and to act as pizza peels or paddles to shoot the pizza into the oven. Pans with a non-stick surface tend to 'stew' doughs – I prefer metal, iron or heavy aluminium. Never use the large pans with perforated bases to make fresh pizzas – these are specifically for reheating bought pizzas and do not work with fresh dough.

Pizza peels or **paddles** are a luxury, but lovely to have and very functional. Wooden peels can act as a serving dish. Metal peels are more practical, although they heat up when they are repeatedly going in and out of the oven and this can make the dough stick to them.

Pizza wheels slice efficiently through a hot pizza without dragging off all the topping.

A **'testo'** or **bakestone** is an affordable luxury if you don't have that outdoor, wood-fired pizza oven. Preheated in the oven for at least 30 minutes before starting to bake, the stone mimics the base of a real pizza oven, and when the uncooked pizza comes into contact with the stone, the moisture is absorbed, the heat evenly distributed and the base will crisp up nicely. There are all types from round to rectangular on the market – some ovens have them as an optional extra. Thick, unglazed quarry/terracotta tiles are a good alternative – use them to line a shelf in the oven. They can be any size, as long as they fit together.

Having tested and cooked all sorts of doughs in all types of ovens, I have found that pizza cooks best in a **standard electric oven** which can reach temperatures of more than 200°C (400°F) Gas 6, and ideally, 220°C (425°F) Gas 7. This will cook the base quickly and be as close to the real thing as possible. Although fan-assisted ovens will work for pizza- and focaccia-baking, they tend to dry out the crust before it browns and the crust can be very pale.

A **wood-burning oven** is the ultimate for the truly serious pizza aficionado. One of these will heat to the right temperature and give that all-important smoky taste to the pizza, which comes from the burning wood. A pizza cooked in one of these will take just minutes as the temperature is more than 500°C. Domestic ovens are available (page 142) and could end up being your best friend!

ten pizza pointers

yeast

Whatever yeast you use, it needs moisture and warmth to develop. Make sure the liquid is at the correct temperature – too cold and the dough will rise slowly; too hot and you risk killing the yeast. When a recipe states 'hand-hot water', it should be between 40.5°C (105°F) and 46°C (115°F).

flour

Using fine Italian '0' grade flour gives the best domestic results. Finer '00' grade is used by professionals and will not give a robust crust at home. Unbleached white bread flour, a mix of soft and hard wheats, will give a very good crust. If you are making dough in a hurry, warm the flour in the microwave for 10 seconds before adding the other ingredients. Always have surplus flour on hand to dust your dough, hands, rolling pin and work surface.

dough

When making the dough, remember: the wetter the dough, the better the dough. A stiff, firm dough is difficult to knead and even more difficult to shape. It will have a poor texture and will not rise properly. If kneaded well, the stickiness soon disappears. Always have surplus olive oil on hand for oiling clingfilm, dough, bowls and tins, when required, to stop the dough from sticking.

kneading

If the dough sticks to your hands when kneading, stop and quickly wash your hands then dip them in a little flour to dry them. You will find the dough doesn't stick to clean hands. Kneading should stretch the dough and develop the elastic gluten in the flour – don't be shy in pulling and stretching the dough.

shaping

Starting off with a perfect round ball will make stretching the dough into a circle much easier. Shape each one into a smooth ball and place on a well-floured tea towel to rise. Dredge liberally all over with flour. When risen, flip the balls over onto a work surface (the flour will have stuck to the dough giving it a non-stick base) and roll out.

topping

The cardinal sin in pizza-making is to overwhelm perfectly-made dough with too much topping. This can make it difficult to shoot into the oven and prevents it rising. If any topping drips down the side of the pizza making it wet, it will not rise. Cheese that misses the target will melt and glue the pizza to the bakestone or parchment.

base

If you like pizzas with a good crisp base, and make them often, it is worth investing in a porous bakestone or 'testo'. Some ovens have them as an accessory, but they are cheap to buy. Otherwise a large, heavy baking sheet that will not warp will do. If you have a solid fuel cooker, cook pizzas directly on the base of the hot oven.

baking

The best way to get a pizza into the oven is to roll the dough directly onto non-stick baking parchment and slide this onto a rimless baking sheet or pizza peel. It will then slide onto the preheated 'testo' or baking sheet easily. For the best results, quickly slide out the parchment paper from under the pizza 5 minutes after the pizza has 'set'. This will make sure that the base crisps up.

serving

Always serve a pizza as soon as it is cooked, slip it onto a wooden board and cut it using a pizza wheel, as knives can drag the topping. Leave filled pizzas to cool for 5 minutes before eating as they can burn the mouth!

eating

Pizza is best eaten in the hand – the crust is there to act as a handle! In Naples, pizzas are folded in four and eaten like a huge sandwich in a paper napkin. Eating it with a knife and fork just sends it skimming across the plate!

basic pizza dough

This will make the typical Neapolitan pizza – soft and chewy with a crisp crust or *cornicione*.

25 g fresh yeast, 1 tablespoon dried active baking yeast or 2 teaspoons fast-action dried yeast

½ teaspoon sugar

250 ml hand-hot water

500 g unbleached white bread flour or Italian '0' grade flour, plus extra to dust

1 teaspoon fine sea salt

1 tablespoon olive oil

Makes 2 medium-crust pizzas, 25–30 cm

In a medium bowl, cream the fresh yeast with the sugar and whisk in the hand-hot water. Leave for 10 minutes until frothy. For other yeasts, follow the manufacturer's instructions.

Sift the flour and salt into a large bowl and make a well in the centre. Pour in the yeast mixture, then the olive oil. Mix together with a round-bladed knife, then use your hands until the dough comes together. Tip out onto a lightly floured surface, wash and dry your hands, then knead briskly for 5–10 minutes until smooth, shiny and elastic. (5 minutes for warm hands, 10 minutes for cold hands!) Don't add extra flour at this stage – a wetter dough is better. If you feel the dough is sticky, flour your hands, not the dough. The dough should be quite soft. If it is *really* too soft, knead in a little more flour.

To test if the dough is ready, roll it into a fat sausage, take each end in either hand, lift the dough up and stretch the dough outwards, gently wiggling it up and down – it should stretch out quite easily. If it doesn't, it needs more kneading. Shape the dough into a neat ball. Put in an oiled bowl, cover with clingfilm or a damp tea towel and leave to rise in a warm, draught-free place until doubled in size – about 1½ hours.

Uncover the dough, punch out the air, then tip out onto a lightly floured work surface. Divide into 2 and shape into smooth balls. Place the balls well apart on non-stick baking parchment, cover loosely with clingfilm and leave to rise for 60–90 minutes. Use as desired.

Sicilian pizza dough

Sicilians tend to use the indigenous yellow *farina di semola* (hard wheat flour) which ensures a lighter crust, with lemon juice to add to the lightness and strengthen the dough.

In a medium bowl, cream the fresh yeast with the sugar and whisk in the hand-hot water. Leave for 10 minutes until frothy. For other yeasts, follow the manufacturer's instructions.

Sift the flour and salt into a large bowl and make a well in the centre. Pour in the yeast mixture, olive oil and lemon juice. Mix until the dough comes together. Add more water if necessary – the dough should be very soft. Tip out onto a lightly floured surface, wash and dry your hands, then knead briskly for at least 10 minutes until smooth, shiny, and elastic. It takes longer to knead this type of dough. Don't add extra flour at this stage – a wetter dough is better. If you feel the dough is sticky, flour your hands, not the dough. The dough should be quite soft. If it is *really* too soft, knead in a little more flour.

To test if the dough is ready, roll it into a fat sausage, take each end in either hand, lift the dough up and stretch the dough outwards, gently wiggling it up and down – it should stretch out quite easily. If it doesn't, it needs more kneading. Shape the dough into a neat ball. Put in an oiled bowl, cover with clingfilm or a damp tea towel and leave to rise in a warm, draught-free place until doubled in size – about 1½ hours.

Uncover the dough, punch out the air, then tip out onto a lightly floured work surface. Divide into 2 and shape into smooth balls. Place the balls well apart on non-stick baking parchment, cover loosely with clingfilm and leave to rise for 60–90 minutes. Use as desired.

10 g fresh yeast, 1 teaspoon dried active baking yeast or ½ teaspoon fast-action dried yeast

a pinch of sugar

150 ml hand-hot water

250 g fine semolina flour (*farina di semola*) or durum wheat flour

½ teaspoon fine sea salt

1 tablespoon olive oil

1 tablespoon freshly squeezed lemon juice

Makes 2 thin-crust pizzas, 20–25 cm

making focaccia

Focaccias are found in many different guises all over Italy, and can be thin and crisp, thick and soft, round or square. I make this deep one in a round tin but it can be made in any shape you wish and cooked on a baking sheet. Although focaccia dough is softer and has a good deal of olive oil added to it, the mixing method is the same as pizza dough. Use the recipe for Deep-pan Focaccia on page 86, then follow the steps below to shape your bread.

Follow the recipe on page 86 so that the dough is at the stage where it has risen twice.

Uncover the dough. Push your fingertips into the dough right down to the base of the tin (don't overdo it!), to make deep dimples all over the surface. The dough will deflate slightly. Drizzle very generously with olive oil (about 80 ml) so that the dimples contain little pools of delicious oil.

Top with little sprigs of rosemary leaves and a generous sprinkling of salt.

Re-cover with clingfilm or a damp tea towel and leave the dough to rise to the top of the tins – about 30 minutes.

Resume the recipe on page 86.

sauces

pizzaiola sauce

This is a key ingredient of pizza and gives it its distinctive flavour. It is a speciality of Naples, but is quite common throughout Italy. To acquire its concentrated, almost caramelized flavour, the tomatoes must be fried over a lively heat.

8 tablespoons olive oil

2 garlic cloves, chopped

1 teaspoon dried oregano

two 400-g tins chopped tomatoes (drained and juice reserved) or 800 g fresh tomatoes, halved and cored

sea salt and freshly ground black pepper

Makes about 400 ml

In a large, shallow pan, heat the oil almost to smoking point (a wok is good for this).

Standing back to avoid the spluttering, add the garlic, oregano and tomatoes including the reserved tinned tomato juice (if using). Cook over a fierce heat for 5–8 minutes or until the sauce is thick and glossy. Season.

Pass the sauce through a food mill (mouli) set over a bowl, to remove seeds and skin. You can put the smooth sauce back in the pan to reduce further if you like. Ladle the sauce into the centre of the pizza base and spread it out in a circular motion with the back of a ladle.

Don't stint on the fresh basil here – it is instrumental in making this the most wonderful sauce in the world! Adding a little softened butter at the end gives the pesto a creaminess that will help it coat hot pasta. The texture is ideal when the pesto is pounded by hand, so try it once and you'll never make it in a food processor again! Pesto can be frozen successfully – some suggest leaving out the cheese and beating it in when the pesto has thawed, but I have never had any problems including it in the beginning.

classic pesto genovese

2 garlic cloves

50 g pine nuts

50 g fresh basil leaves

150 ml extra virgin olive oil, plus extra to preserve

50 g unsalted butter, softened

4 tablespoons freshly grated Parmesan cheese

sea salt and freshly ground black pepper

Makes about 250 ml

Peel the garlic and put it in a pestle and mortar with a little salt and the pine nuts. Pound until broken up. Add the basil leaves, a few at a time, pounding and mixing to a paste. Gradually beat in the olive oil, little by little, until the mixture is creamy and thick.

Alternatively, put everything in a food processor and process until just smooth.

Beat in the butter and season with pepper, then beat in the Parmesan. Spoon into a screw top jar with a layer of olive oil on top to exclude the air, then store in the fridge, for up to 2 weeks, until needed.

fiery red pesto

Years ago, long before it appeared on supermarket shelves, I devised this recipe to remind me of the flavours of southern Italy. Needless to say, this tastes really special and you can adjust the heat to your liking. Although not at all Italian, fresh coriander is a fantastic alternative to the basil.

1 large red pepper

50 g fresh basil leaves

1 garlic clove

30 g toasted pine nuts

6 sun-dried tomatoes in oil, drained

2 ripe tomatoes, skinned

3 tablespoons tomato purée

½ teaspoon chilli powder

50 g freshly grated Parmesan cheese

150 ml olive oil, plus extra to preserve

Makes about 350 ml

Preheat the grill to high.

Place the pepper on the grill rack and grill, turning occasionally, until charred all over. Put the pepper in a covered bowl until cool enough to handle, then peel off the skin. Halve and remove the core and seeds.

Place the pepper and the remaining ingredients, except the oil, in a food processor. Process until smooth, then, with the machine running, slowly add the oil. Spoon into a screw-top jar with a layer of olive oil on top to exclude the air, then store in the fridge, for up to 2 weeks, until needed.

black olive and tomato relish

This is a wonderfully useful relish to have sitting in the fridge to spread onto pizza bases or simply to serve with flatbreads as a dip. I always use the wrinkly, oven-dried black olives (sometimes known as Greek-style, but not kalamata) as they have a good, rich flavour.

2 tablespoons sun-dried tomato oil

1 red onion, peeled and diced

1 garlic clove, peeled and crushed

5 plump sun-dried tomatoes in oil, drained and diced

250 g stoned black (or oven-dried) olives

1 fresh bay leaf

15 fresh basil leaves, torn into pieces

freshly squeezed juice of 1 lemon

3–4 tablespoons extra virgin olive oil, plus extra to preserve

sea salt and freshly ground black pepper

Makes about 350 g

In a medium saucepan, heat the sun-dried tomato oil and gently sweat the onion and garlic for a few minutes. Add the sun-dried tomatoes, olives and bay leaf and continue to cook for a few minutes until the flavours have melded.

Season, remove from the heat and discard the bay leaf. Pour the mixture into a food processor with the basil and process until you have a coarse purée. (You may have to do this in 2 batches if there isn't enough room in the food processor.) Add the lemon juice, oil and more seasoning, if necessary.

Spoon into a screw-top jar with a layer of olive oil on top to exclude the air, then store in the fridge, for up to 2 weeks, until needed.

pizzas thick and thin

A Neapolitan baker called Raffaele Esposito is said to have been responsible for the birth of modern-day pizza. In 1889, in Naples, he baked three different pizzas for the visit of King Umberto I and Queen Margherita of Savoy. The Queen's favourite was very patriotic, symbolizing the flag of newly unified Italy in its colours of green (basil leaves), white (mozzarella) and red (tomatoes). It was then named Pizza Margherita in her honour and this is it. To be truly authentic, all the ingredients should be local – the basil should really be hand-picked from a Neapolitan balcony!

pizza margherita

½ recipe Basic Pizza Dough (page 12), making just 1 ball of dough

3–4 tablespoons Pizzaiola Sauce (page 17)

50–75 g buffalo mozzarella or cow's milk mozzarella (*fior di latte*)

200 g very ripe cherry tomatoes, halved

a good handful of fresh basil leaves

extra virgin olive oil, to drizzle

sea salt and freshly ground black pepper

a testo, terracotta bakestone or a large, heavy baking sheet

a pizza peel or rimless baking sheet

Makes 1 medium-crust pizza, 25–35 cm

Put the testo, terracotta bakestone or a large, heavy baking sheet on the lower shelf of the oven. Preheat the oven to 220°C (425°F) Gas 7 for at least 30 minutes.

Lightly squeeze any excess moisture out of the mozzarella, then roughly slice it.

Uncover the dough, punch out the air and roll or pull into a 25-cm circle directly onto non-stick baking parchment. Slide this onto the pizza peel or rimless baking sheet. Spread the pizzaiola sauce over the pizza base, leaving a 1-cm rim around the edge. Scatter with the tomatoes and season.

Working quickly, open the oven door and slide paper and pizza onto the hot bakestone or baking sheet. If you are brave, try to shoot the pizza into the oven so that it leaves the paper behind – this takes practice!

Bake for 5 minutes, remove from the oven and scatter the mozzarella over the tomatoes. Return the pizza to the oven without the paper. Bake for a further 15 minutes or until the crust is golden and the cheese melted but still white. Remove from the oven, scatter with the basil leaves and drizzle with olive oil. Eat immediately.

This is *the* classic pizza and it is always made without mozzarella. According to Neapolitans, when anchovies are added, it is transformed into a Pizza Romana. Dried oregano is preferable to fresh, as it is much more fragrant, especially if you crush it between your fingers before sprinkling over the pizza. In Italy, wild oregano is sold in thick bunches, dries out in a matter of days and is rubbed straight off the bunch into whatever's cooking.

pizza marinara

½ recipe Basic Pizza Dough (page 12), making just 1 ball of dough

3–4 tablespoons Pizzaiola Sauce (page 17)

200 g very ripe tomatoes, sliced and deseeded

2 garlic cloves, thinly sliced

1 teaspoon dried oregano

extra virgin olive oil, to drizzle

a few sprigs fresh oregano

sea salt and freshly ground black pepper

a testo, terracotta bakestone or a large, heavy baking sheet

a pizza peel or rimless baking sheet

Makes 1 medium-crust pizza, 25–35 cm

Put the testo, terracotta bakestone or a large, heavy baking sheet on the lower shelf of the oven. Preheat the oven to 220°C (425°F) Gas 7 for at least 30 minutes.

Uncover the dough, punch out the air and roll or pull into a 25-cm circle directly onto non-stick baking parchment. Slide this onto the pizza peel or rimless baking sheet. Spread the pizzaiola sauce over the pizza base, leaving a 1-cm rim around the edge. Scatter with the tomatoes and garlic, sprinkle with the dried oregano, drizzle with olive oil, then season.

Working quickly, open the oven door and slide paper and pizza onto the hot bakestone or baking sheet. If you are brave, try to shoot the pizza into the oven so that it leaves the paper behind – this takes practice!

Bake for 5 minutes, then carefully slide out the baking parchment. Bake the pizza for a further 15 minutes, or until the crust is golden. Remove from the oven, scatter with the fresh oregano and drizzle with olive oil. Eat immediately.

This is quite a substantial pizza, and can be as fiery and angry as you like – it's up to you how much chilli you put in. I love this with fresh Italian sausage meat, but you could use thick slices of *salame piccante* or even a hot merguez or chorizo. Chilled beer is an essential accompaniment.

angry pizza
pizza arrabiata

½ recipe Basic Pizza Dough (page 12), making just 1 ball of dough

50–75 g buffalo mozzarella or cow's milk mozzarella (*fior di latte*)

200 g (about 6) plum tomatoes, halved

150 g fresh spicy sausage, sliced or removed from the skin and crumbled

50 g Peppadew peppers

½ teaspoon fennel seeds

red chilli flakes, to taste

chilli oil or extra virgin olive oil, to drizzle

sea salt and freshly ground black pepper

a testo, terracotta bakestone or a large, heavy baking sheet

a pizza peel or rimless baking sheet

Makes 1 medium-crust pizza, 25–35 cm

Put the testo, terracotta bakestone or a large, heavy baking sheet on the lower shelf of the oven. Preheat the oven to 220°C (425°F) Gas 7 for at least 30 minutes.

Lightly squeeze any excess moisture out of the mozzarella, then slice or chop into cubes.

Uncover the dough, punch out the air and roll or pull into a 25-cm circle directly onto non-stick baking parchment. Slide this onto the pizza peel or rimless baking sheet.

Arrange the tomatoes over the pizza base leaving a 1-cm rim around the edge. Scatter with the sausage, then the Peppadew peppers, then the mozzarella. Sprinkle with the fennel seeds and chilli flakes, then season. Working quickly, open the oven door and slide paper and pizza onto the hot bakestone or baking sheet. If you are brave, try to shoot the pizza into the oven so that it leaves the paper behind – this takes practice!

Bake for 5 minutes, then slide out the baking parchment if possible. Bake for a further 15 minutes or until the crust is golden and the cheese melted but still white. Remove from the oven and drizzle with the chilli oil. Eat immediately.

Neapolitans naturally call pizza without tomatoes Pizza Bianca. All the flavour comes from the mozzarella, so this *has* to be the finest buffalo mozzarella. This cheese tends to be quite wet, so squeeze out any watery whey before slicing it. I like to add sage to the pizza – its muskiness beautifully complements the milky mozzarella.

pizza bianca

½ recipe Basic Pizza Dough (page 12), making just 1 ball of dough

100 g buffalo mozzarella or cow's milk mozzarella (*fior di latte*)

a handful of small fresh sage leaves

extra virgin olive oil, to drizzle

sea salt and freshly ground black pepper

a testo, terracotta bakestone or a large, heavy baking sheet

a pizza peel or rimless baking sheet

Makes 1 medium-crust pizza, 25–35 cm

Put the testo, terracotta bakestone or a large, heavy baking sheet on the lower shelf of the oven. Preheat the oven to 220°C (425°F) Gas 7 for at least 30 minutes.

Lightly squeeze any excess moisture out of the mozzarella, then slice it and put it on kitchen paper for 5 minutes to absorb any remaining moisture.

Uncover the dough, punch out the air and roll or pull into a 25-cm circle directly onto non-stick baking parchment. Slide this onto the pizza peel or rimless baking sheet. Arrange the mozzarella evenly over the pizza base, leaving a 1-cm rim around the edge. Scatter the sage over the cheese, then season and drizzle with olive oil.

Working quickly, open the oven door and slide paper and pizza onto the hot bakestone or baking sheet. If you are brave, try to shoot the pizza into the oven so that it leaves the paper behind – this takes practice!

Bake for 5 minutes, then carefully slide out the baking parchment. Bake the pizza for a further 15 minutes, or until the crust is golden and the cheese melted and bubbling. Remove from the oven and sprinkle with freshly ground black pepper. Eat immediately.

This makes a change from the normal scattering of token sliced mushrooms: here we have fresh mushrooms in all their glory, under a crispy garlicky topping of breadcrumbs and Parmesan. Don't use button mushrooms for this – they often have little or no taste at all. Chestnut or other large, dark open mushrooms are ideal.

garlic mushroom pizza
pizza ai funghi e aglio

½ recipe Basic Pizza Dough (page 12), making just 1 ball of dough

50–75 g buffalo mozzarella or cow's milk mozzarella (*fior di latte*)

50 g fresh breadcrumbs

30 g freshly grated Parmesan cheese

4 garlic cloves, finely chopped

4 tablespoons chopped fresh parsley

30 g butter, melted

about 12 medium chestnut mushrooms

extra virgin olive oil, to drizzle

sea salt and freshly ground black pepper

a testo, terracotta bakestone or a large, heavy baking sheet

a pizza peel or rimless baking sheet

Makes 1 medium-crust pizza, 25–35 cm

Put the testo, terracotta bakestone or a large, heavy baking sheet on the lower shelf of the oven. Preheat the oven to 220°C (425°F) Gas 7 for at least 30 minutes.

Lightly squeeze any excess moisture out of the mozzarella, then slice or chop into cubes. Mix the breadcrumbs with the Parmesan, garlic and parsley then stir in the melted butter. Lightly fill the cavities of the mushrooms with the breadcrumb mixture.

Uncover the dough, punch out the air and roll or pull into a 25-cm circle directly onto non-stick baking parchment. Slide this onto the pizza peel or rimless baking sheet. Arrange the mozzarella over the pizza base leaving a 2-cm rim around the edge. Arrange the stuffed mushrooms all over, sprinkling any remaining breadcrumbs over the finished pizza. Drizzle with olive oil and season.

Working quickly, open the oven door and slide paper and pizza onto the hot bakestone or baking sheet. If you are brave, try to shoot the pizza into the oven so that it leaves the paper behind – this takes practice!

Bake for 5 minutes, then slide out the baking parchment if possible (this will be quite difficult with the wobbly mushrooms). Bake for a further 15 minutes or until the crust is golden, the cheese melted and the mushrooms tender and bubbling. Remove from the oven and drizzle with olive oil. Eat immediately.

With no hint of tomato sauce, this is a succulent pizza where the onions are cooked until soft and caramelized, before being spread on the pizza on top of the mozzarella. Olives, capers and anchovies add savouriness to the sweet onions. You may leave out the anchovies and add tuna or sardines instead.

caramelized red onion pizza with capers and olives
pizza con cipolle rosse, capperi e olive

1 recipe Basic Pizza Dough (page 12), dividing the dough into 6–8 balls

1 kg red onions, finely sliced

freshly squeezed juice of 1 lemon

4 tablespoons olive oil, plus extra to drizzle

2 teaspoons dried oregano

1 mozzarella, drained and thinly sliced

2 tablespoons freshly grated Parmesan cheese

12 anchovy fillets in oil, drained (optional)

15 black olives, stoned

2 tablespoons capers in salt, washed and drained

sea salt and freshly ground black pepper

two testi, terracotta bakestones or large, heavy baking sheets

2 rimless baking sheets

Makes 4–6 pizzas, depending on size

Put the testi, terracotta bakestones or large, heavy baking sheets on the lower shelf of the oven. Preheat the oven to 220°C (425°F) Gas 7 for at least 30 minutes.

Toss the onions in the lemon juice to coat them thoroughly. Heat the oil in a large, shallow saucepan and add the onions. Cook over a gentle heat for about 10 minutes, stirring occasionally, until they are beginning to colour. Stir in the dried oregano.

Uncover the dough balls, punch out the air and roll or pull each one into thin circles directly onto separate sheets of non-stick baking parchment. Slide these onto 2 rimless baking sheets.

Cover the pizza bases with the mozzarella leaving a 1-cm rim around the edge. Top with the onions and sprinkle with the Parmesan. Scatter the anchovy fillets, olives and capers over the top. Drizzle with olive oil, then season, but don't use too much salt as the capers will be salty.

Working quickly, open the oven door, and slide paper and pizzas onto the hot bakestones or baking sheets. Bake for 15–20 minutes or until the crust is golden. Remove from the oven and drizzle with olive oil. Eat immediately.

Using the plumpest raw prawns you can find will ensure that they don't toughen up through over-cooking. Avoid using pre-cooked prawns which will make the end result dry, chewy and unappetizing. If you do have to use the pre-cooked variety, pop them onto the pizza 5 minutes from the end of cooking time.

Sicilian prawn and tomato pizza
pizza ai gamberoni di Sicilia

½ recipe Sicilian Pizza Dough (page 14), making just 1 ball of dough

3–4 tablespoons Pizzaiola Sauce (page 17)

3 garlic cloves, sliced thinly

½ teaspoon red chilli flakes

10–12 medium uncooked prawns, tail shells still attached

200 g very ripe cherry tomatoes or any other very tasty small tomatoes

a good handful of fresh flat leaf parsley, roughly chopped

extra virgin olive oil, to drizzle

sea salt and freshly ground black pepper

lemon wedges, to serve

a testo, terracotta bakestone or a large, heavy baking sheet

a pizza peel or rimless baking sheet

Makes 1 medium-crust pizza, 25–35 cm

Put the testo, terracotta bakestone or a large, heavy baking sheet on the lower shelf of the oven. Preheat the oven to 220°C (425°F) Gas 7 for at least 30 minutes.

Uncover the dough, punch out the air and roll or pull into a 25-cm circle directly onto non-stick baking parchment. Slide this onto the pizza peel or rimless baking sheet. Spread the pizzaiola sauce over the pizza base, leaving a 1-cm rim around the edge. Scatter with the garlic, chilli flakes, prawns and tomatoes. Season.

Working quickly, open the oven door and slide paper and pizza onto the hot bakestone or baking sheet. If you are brave, try to shoot the pizza into the oven so that it leaves the paper behind – this takes practice!

Bake for 5 minutes, then carefully slide out the baking parchment. Bake the pizza for a further 15 minutes, or until the crust is golden and the prawns cooked. Remove from the oven, scatter with the parsley and drizzle with olive oil. Eat immediately with the lemon wedges for squeezing over the pizza.

This is a real favourite of mine. I use very thinly sliced smoked pancetta (the Italian equivalent of streaky bacon, made from salt-cured pork belly). Pancetta comes in many forms: in whole cured slabs (with or without herbs and spices), smoked or unsmoked, or rolled up for slicing thinly, aged or not. The choice is endless and varies from region to region. Outside Italy, you can buy the smoked slab with rind, ready-sliced smoked or rolled unsmoked pancetta. Combined with Fiery Red Pesto, this is incredible!

pizza con pancetta

1 recipe Basic Pizza Dough (page 12)

6 tablespoons Fiery Red Pesto (page 20)

24 thin slices pancetta or thin streaky bacon

extra virgin olive oil, to drizzle

sea salt and freshly ground black pepper

a testo, terracotta bakestone or a large, heavy baking sheet

a pizza peel or rimless baking sheet

Makes 1 medium-crust pizza, approximately 20 x 40 cm

Put the testo, terracotta bakestone or a large, heavy baking sheet on the lower shelf of the oven. Preheat the oven to 220°C (425°F) Gas 7 for at least 30 minutes.

Uncover the dough, punch out the air and roll or pull into a rectangle, about 20 cm wide and as long as your oven will take (you can always make 2 shorter ones). Roll the dough directly onto non-stick baking parchment. Slide this onto the pizza peel or rimless baking sheet.

Spread the red pesto over the pizza base, leaving a 1-cm rim around the edge. Lay the strips of pancetta widthways across the pizza – they should be almost the same width as the dough. Season and drizzle with oil.

Working quickly, open the oven door and slide paper and pizza onto the hot bakestone or baking sheet. If you are brave, try to shoot the pizza into the oven so that it leaves the paper behind – this takes practice!

Bake for 5 minutes, then carefully slide out the baking parchment. Bake the pizza for a further 15 minutes, or until the crust is golden and the pancetta crisp. Remove from the oven and drizzle with olive oil. Cut into fingers and eat immediately.

Artichokes preserved in oil for antipasti are perfect for pizza-making as the delicious oil they are soaked in means they won't dry out during cooking. I have also made this with smoked mozzarella and it is equally delicious.

pizza with artichokes and mozzarella
pizza ai carciofi e scamorza

½ recipe Basic Pizza Dough (page 12), making just 1 ball of dough

100 g buffalo mozzarella or cow's milk mozzarella (*fior di latte*)

100 g artichokes preserved in oil (or grilled artichokes from a deli)

1–2 garlic cloves, finely chopped

2 tablespoons extra virgin olive oil, plus extra to drizzle

6–8 juicy black olives

2 tablespoons roughly chopped fresh flat leaf parsley

sea salt and freshly ground black pepper

a testo, terracotta bakestone or a large, heavy baking sheet

a pizza peel or rimless baking sheet

Makes 1 medium-crust pizza, 25–35 cm, or 2 small pizzas

Put the testo, terracotta bakestone or a large, heavy baking sheet on the lower shelf of the oven. Preheat the oven to 220°C (425°F) Gas 7 for at least 30 minutes.

Lightly squeeze any excess moisture out of the mozzarella, then slice it and leave the slices on kitchen paper for 5 minutes to absorb any remaining moisture. Cut the artichokes into quarters and toss them with the garlic and olive oil.

Uncover the dough, punch out the air and roll or pull into a 25-cm circle directly onto non-stick baking parchment. Slide this onto the pizza peel or rimless baking sheet. Arrange the mozzarella evenly over the pizza base, leaving a 1-cm rim around the edge. Scatter the artichoke and olives over the mozzarella, then season and drizzle with olive oil.

Working quickly, open the oven door and slide paper and pizza onto the hot bakestone or baking sheet. If you are brave, try to shoot the pizza into the oven so that it leaves the paper behind – this takes practice!

Bake for 5 minutes, then carefully slide out the baking parchment. Bake the pizza for a further 15 minutes, or until the crust is golden and the cheese melted and bubbling. Remove from the oven and sprinkle the parsley and freshly ground pepper over the top. Eat immediately.

This contains all the heat of southern Italy. *Provolone piccante*, originally from Campania, is a sharp, aged cow's cheese often found in a globe shape and usually covered in a waxed rind. It makes a delicious sandwich with fresh tomato, dried oregano and a drizzle of olive oil.

pizza piccante

½ recipe Sicilian Pizza Dough (page 14), making just 1 ball of dough

4 tablespoons Pizzaiola Sauce (page 17)

50 g buffalo mozzarella or cow's milk mozzarella (*fior di latte*)

3 large garlic cloves, thinly sliced

50 g *provolone piccante*, thinly sliced

2 fat red chillies (or more), thinly sliced

extra virgin olive oil, to drizzle

chilli oil, to drizzle

sea salt and freshly crushed black pepper

a testo, terracotta bakestone or a large, heavy baking sheet

a pizza peel or rimless baking sheet

Makes 1 medium-crust pizza, 25–35 cm

Put the testo, terracotta bakestone or a large, heavy baking sheet on the lower shelf of the oven. Preheat the oven to 220°C (425°F) Gas 7 for at least 30 minutes.

Lightly squeeze any excess moisture out of the mozzarella, then slice it and leave the slices on kitchen paper for 5 minutes to absorb any remaining moisture.

Uncover the dough, punch out the air and roll or pull into a 25-cm circle directly onto non-stick baking parchment. Slide this onto the pizza peel or rimless baking sheet. Spread the pizzaiola sauce over the pizza base, leaving a 1-cm rim around the edge. Scatter the garlic over the top. Arrange the provolone and mozzarella on top and scatter with the chillies. Season well with plenty of crushed black pepper and drizzle with olive oil.

Working quickly, open the oven door and slide paper and pizza onto the hot bakestone or baking sheet. If you are brave, try to shoot the pizza into the oven so that it leaves the paper behind – this takes practice!

Bake for 5 minutes, then carefully slide out the baking parchment. Bake the pizza for a further 15 minutes, or until the crust is golden and the cheese melted and bubbling. Remove from the oven and drizzle with the chilli oil. Eat immediately.

Schiacciate (skee-a-chah-tay) in Tuscany are individual thin, crispy pizzas with the simplest of toppings. Forget Neapolitan pizzas – the dough is rolled out to almost baking-parchment thinness, laid on an oiled tray, then topped with cheese, vegetables and prosciutto, all of which are cut wafer-thin so that they will cook quickly. Mozzarella is often used as the base instead of tomato sauce, and sliced fresh tomatoes or halved cherry tomatoes are scattered on top of the cheese. Fresh herbs or a handful of peppery rocket are often added when the pizza comes sizzling out of the oven.

little Tuscan pizzas
schiacciate Toscana

1 recipe Basic Pizza Dough (page 12)

Choose from the following toppings (thinly slice any vegetables and mozzarella):

salami, red onion and capers

aubergine, red onions, mozzarella and sage

potato, mozzarella, anchovy, olive, sage or rosemary

courgette, mozzarella, anchovy and basil

mozzarella, tomato and rocket

extra virgin olive oil, to drizzle

sea salt and freshly ground black pepper

2 heavy baking sheets

Makes 6 small, thin pizzas

Place 2 heavy baking sheets in the oven. Preheat the oven to 220°C (425°F) Gas 7 for at least 30 minutes.

Uncover the dough, punch out the air and divide into 6. Shape each piece into a smooth ball and roll into a very thin circle. Put the discs on a couple of baking sheets lined with non-stick baking parchment. Arrange a few slices of mozzarella on top (if using). Toss the chosen sliced vegetables in a little olive oil and arrange sparingly on top of the pizza bases along with any other toppings.

Working quickly, open the oven door and slide paper and pizzas onto the hot baking sheets. Bake the pizzas for 15–20 minutes, or until the crust is golden and crisp. Remove from the oven, scatter with any herbs, drizzle with olive oil and serve immediately.

This is a sort of new-wave pizza, and very popular in Italian city pizzerias. Soft, buttery Taleggio, made in the valleys and mountains of Lombardy and the Valtellina, melts and runs very quickly, so make sure it's not near the edge of the pizza. Ripe, juicy pear is the perfect foil for this cheese, and don't leave out the sage – it's integral to the flavour.

pear, pecorino and Taleggio pizza with honey and sage
pizza con pere, pecorino, Taleggio, salvia e miele

½ recipe Basic Pizza Dough (page 12), making just 1 ball of dough

2 tablespoons extra virgin olive oil, plus extra to drizzle

125 g Taleggio (rind removed), cubed

1 very ripe pear, cored and thinly sliced

12–15 small sage leaves

50 g freshly grated pecorino cheese

1 tablespoon runny honey (acacia or orange blossom, if possible)

sea salt and freshly ground black pepper

a testo, terracotta bakestone or a large, heavy baking sheet

a pizza peel or rimless baking sheet

Makes 1 medium-crust pizza, 25–35 cm

Put the testo, terracotta bakestone or a large, heavy baking sheet on the lower shelf of the oven. Preheat the oven to 220°C (425°F) Gas 7 for at least 30 minutes.

Uncover the dough, punch out the air and roll or pull into a 25-cm circle directly onto non-stick baking parchment. Slide this onto the pizza peel or rimless baking sheet. Rub the pizza base with the olive oil and scatter over the Taleggio. Arrange the pears over this, then the sage and pecorino. Drizzle with the honey, then season and drizzle with a little more olive oil.

Working quickly, open the oven door and slide paper and pizza onto the hot bakestone or baking sheet. If you are brave, try to shoot the pizza into the oven so that it leaves the paper behind – this takes practice!

Bake for 5 minutes, then carefully slide out the baking parchment. Bake the pizza for a further 15 minutes, or until the crust is golden and the cheese melted and bubbling. Sprinkle with freshly ground black pepper and eat immediately.

You will see mounds of this thick pizza on food stalls all over Palermo. It is the ultimate snack on the run and is perfect for picnics and lunchboxes. It may seem strange, but in Sicily, breadcrumbs are sprinkled over pasta and even on top of pizza. Very often this dough is made in two stages: a loose batter is made and left to rise, then the remaining ingredients are kneaded in and left to rise again, but my method reduces the time. Make sure you use good olive oil here.

Palermo pizza
sfinciune

2 recipes Sicilian Pizza Dough (page 14), making the changes stated in this recipe

7 tablespoons olive oil, plus extra to drizzle

1 large onion, sliced

3 large ripe tomatoes, chopped

1 teaspoon dried oregano, plus extra to taste

8 anchovy fillets in oil, drained and chopped

75 g dried breadcrumbs

75 g *caciocavallo* (or Emmental), cubed

sea salt and freshly ground black pepper

a rectangular baking tin, 35 x 25 x 3 cm, oiled

a testo, terracotta bakestone or a large, heavy baking sheet

Makes 1 thick pizza, 35 x 25 cm

When you make the pizza dough, replace the lemon juice with olive oil. Rise once, then punch down the air, knead lightly and roll or pull into a rectangle that will fit into the prepared baking tin. Cover the tin lightly with clingfilm or a damp tea towel and leave in a warm place to rise until it has reached the top of the tin (about 30 minutes).

While the dough is rising, put the testo, terracotta bakestone or a large, heavy baking sheet on the lower shelf of the oven. Preheat the oven to 220°C (425°F) Gas 7 for at least 30 minutes.

To make the sauce, heat 4 tablespoons of the olive oil in a saucepan and add the onion. Cook until soft but not coloured, then add the tomatoes, dried oregano and anchovy fillets. Cook for 5 minutes until the anchovies dissolve and the tomatoes collapse. Season to taste.

Heat the remaining olive oil in a frying pan and fry the breadcrumbs until golden and crisp.

When the dough has risen, uncover and dimple the top lightly with your fingers as if you were making focaccia, but don't make too many holes. Spread with half of the sauce and bake for 25 minutes.

Remove from the oven, spread the remaining sauce over the top, scatter over the breadcrumbs and extra oregano and drizzle with olive oil. Finish by scattering the caciocavallo over everything, then bake for another 5 minutes until the top is golden. Serve warm or cold, cut into squares.

Schiacciata is a dialect word meaning 'flattened', so pizza is sometimes known as schiacciata, i.e. a flattened bread dough. After making pizza one day, I had some dough left over and devised this 'pizza' using leftover olives. There is no olive oil needed here, but you can have some really good oil in a little pot ready for dipping the hot pizzas into. Alternatively, you could pile on some Black Olive and Tomato Relish (page 20) as the schiacciate come out of the oven.

crispy olive 'pizza'
schiacciata croccante con olive

any leftover Basic Pizza Dough
(page 12)

a splash of white wine

a handful of green olives, stoned and
roughly chopped

rock salt

extra virgin olive oil or Black Olive and
Tomato Relish (page 20), to serve

*a testo, terracotta bakestone or a
large, heavy baking sheet*

a large rimless baking sheet

Put the testo, terracotta bakestone or a large, heavy baking sheet on the lower shelf of the oven. Preheat the oven to 220°C (425°F) Gas 7 for at least 30 minutes.

Using a rolling pin, roll the dough out as thinly as you can, directly onto the baking sheet. Brush the dough with a little white wine, scatter with the olives and sprinkle with rock salt. Lightly press the olives and salt into the dough. Using a pizza wheel, score the dough in lozenge shapes directly on the baking sheet.

Bake for 5–10 minutes until the schiacciate are puffed and pale golden. Remove from the oven and break up into the pre-cut lozenges. Serve warm with olive oil or Black Olive and Tomato Relish.

Although not crispy like a pizza, this is a wonderful alternative for those who love mashed potato or who are wheat-intolerant, and it is popular in southern Italian homes. If you are not keen on anchovies, try using tinned tuna – you can really try any pizza topping you like, even mozzarella. Have some pizzaiola sauce to serve on the side, along with barbecued sausages for any meat-eaters. Other recipes for potato pizza incorporate mashed potato in normal pizza dough, which is delicious, but a little heavy, and obviously not wheat-free!

potato pizza
pizza di patate

750 g floury-fleshed potatoes (King Edwards, Golden Wonder, Red Rooster), unpeeled

2 tablespoons olive oil, plus extra to drizzle

6–8 cherry or baby plum tomatoes, halved

50 g black wrinkly olives, stones in

25 g salted capers, rinsed

3 salted anchovies, rinsed

1 small red onion, sliced into thin rings and tossed in olive oil

1 teaspoon dried oregano

sea salt and freshly ground black pepper

a shallow sandwich tin or pizza pan, 23 cm, oiled

Makes 1 pizza, 23 cm

Preheat the oven to 200°C (400°F) Gas 6.

Boil the potatoes in plenty of salted water until tender. Drain well and carefully peel off the skins. Mash the potatoes or push them through a potato ricer, then leave to cool for 5 minutes. Beat in the olive oil and season to taste. Spoon into the prepared sandwich tin or pizza pan and smooth out the surface.

Top with the tomatoes, olives, capers, anchovies and onion rings. Sprinkle with the dried oregano and drizzle with olive oil. Bake in the oven for 20 minutes until sizzling. Serve hot or cold.

This wheat-free pizza is very good, but don't expect a pizza-like dough. It starts life as a batter and when baked, becomes chewy and sponge-like on the inside, with a crisp crust. I've suggested a very reliable gluten-free flour (a mix of rice, potato and tapioca flours blended with xanthan gum) and developed this recipe for those who can't eat wheat but still crave that unique pizza experience. You could also try mixing in other gluten-free flours, such as chickpea or buckwheat.

½ aubergine, cubed

1 small red pepper, deseeded and cut into strips

1 small courgette, sliced

2 garlic cloves, sliced

6 tablespoons olive oil, plus extra to drizzle

40 ml each milk and water, mixed together and warmed

¾ teaspoon freshly squeezed lemon juice

1 egg

½ teaspoon salt

225 g gluten-free white bread flour, such as Dove's Farm

1 teaspoon fast-action dried yeast

75 g mozzarella, drained and cubed (optional)

sea salt and freshly ground black pepper

a shallow pizza pan, 23 cm, oiled

Makes 1 pizza, 23 cm

wheat-free pizza with roasted vegetables

Preheat the oven to 200°C (400°F) Gas 6.

Toss the aubergine, red pepper, courgette and garlic in 4 tablespoons of the olive oil and roast on a roasting tray in the oven for 15–20 minutes, or until they are beginning to soften.

While the vegetables are roasting, make the batter. Whisk the warm (not hot) milk and water, the lemon juice, remaining olive oil, egg and salt together. Beat in the flour and yeast and mix until well combined. Pour into the prepared pizza pan, cover and leave to rise in a warm place for about 20 minutes or until puffy.

Bake the pizza base in the oven for 10 minutes to set the dough, then quickly remove from the oven and scatter with the roasted vegetables and mozzarella (if using). Season well, drizzle with olive oil and return to the oven for a further 10 minutes until the vegetables are sizzling and the pizza has slightly shrunk from the edges. Cut into wedges and serve hot.

A *piadina* ('little plate') is traditionally cooked on a testo (a thick, flat piece of terracotta, see page 9). As these are difficult to buy outside Italy, I use unglazed terracotta plant-pot saucers with great success. Never oil a testo – it must be clean and dry. Heat it gently over a low gas flame or an electric ring, gradually increasing the heat to medium. Alternatively, use an iron girdle or a heavy-based frying pan, but make sure it is hot before using it. Keep the piadine warm and soft inside a folded napkin in a basket until they are ready to serve. Serve them warm, folded over, with thinly sliced prosciutto crudo or salami piled inside.

flatbreads from Emilia Romagna
piadine

500 g Italian '00' flour or plain white flour (NOT strong bread flour)

1 teaspoon baking powder

a pinch of fine sea salt

4 tablespoons good olive oil, melted unsalted butter or pure lard (*strutto*)

200 ml hand-hot water

a testo, iron girdle or heavy-based frying pan

Makes about 8 flatbreads

Sift the flour, baking powder and salt into a large bowl. Make a well in the centre and pour in the oil and the hand-hot water to make a soft dough. Add more water if the dough looks dry. Knead for a couple of minutes or until smooth, wrap in clingfilm and leave to rest at room temperature for 30 minutes. (Alternatively, you can make the dough the day before and refrigerate it.)

Divide the dough into 8, keeping the pieces covered under an upturned bowl. Roll each into a thin 20-cm disc. Stack these up with non-stick baking parchment or clingfilm between each, and cover with clingfilm or a damp tea towel.

Heat the testo on the hob until medium hot. Slide a disc onto the hot testo and cook for 30–40 seconds until brown spots appear on the underside. Flip it over and cook for a further 30 seconds or until both sides are dry-looking and covered with brown spots or blisters (like a Mexican tortilla or Indian chappati). Avoid cooking them for too long as they will end up being dry and tough.

Keep the cooked piadine warm and soft inside a folded napkin or loosely wrapped in aluminium foil in a warm oven while you are cooking the remainder. They are best served warm.

Farinata is a Ligurian speciality and should be made with very good olive oil. It is traditionally baked in a large, shallow copper pan, but a wide metal pizza pan will do. It is often cut into lozenge shapes and eaten as a snack. I like to make it into a type of pizza for those who can't eat wheat: I cook it for 10 minutes or until just set, strew prawns, tomatoes and diced pancetta on top, then cook until firm and golden. The batter itself can be flavoured with chopped rosemary, dried chilli or black pepper. If you can't find Italian chickpea flour, use Indian gram flour (available in Asian food stores) although the colour will be paler.

chickpea and rosemary flatbread
farinata

4 tablespoons extra virgin olive oil

200 g Italian chickpea flour or gram flour

1 teaspoon sea salt, plus extra to sprinkle

4 sprigs of fresh rosemary, leaves stripped off

freshly ground black pepper

a pizza pan, 28 cm, preferably non-stick

Makes 1 flatbread, 28 cm

Put 500 ml cold water in a bowl with 1 tablespoon of the olive oil. Gradually whisk in the chickpea flour and salt until smooth and creamy. Cover and leave to stand for at least 30 minutes, or overnight in the fridge if possible.

Preheat the oven to 220°C (425°F) Gas 7 or hotter, if possible.

Oil the pizza pan with the remaining olive oil. It must be well oiled to give the right flavour and ensure a crisp edge.

Stir the batter and pour into the prepared pizza pan. Sprinkle the rosemary on top and bake for about 20 minutes or until set and golden. Serve warm, cut into slices or lozenge shapes, and sprinkled with salt and pepper.

calzones and pizza pies

This is a good calzone to make for more than two people. The filling ingredients can be chopped as finely or roughly as you like, but the aubergine must be cooked through before it goes into the dough. I sometimes add a couple of tablespoons of pizzaiola sauce to the mixture to make it extra tomatoey.

calzone alla parmigiana

1 recipe Basic Pizza Dough (page 12), up to the first rising

2 aubergines, cubed

12 whole garlic cloves, peeled

4 tablespoons extra virgin olive oil, plus extra to glaze

200 g buffalo mozzarella or cow's milk mozzarella (*fior di latte*)

5 ripe tomatoes, cubed

3 tablespoons chopped fresh basil

4 tablespoons freshly grated Parmesan cheese

sea salt and freshly ground black pepper

2 large, heavy baking sheets
2 rimless baking sheets

Makes 4 calzone

Put the baking sheets into the oven. Preheat the oven to 200°C (400°F) Gas 6 for at least 30 minutes.

Uncover the dough, punch out the air and divide into 4 balls. Dredge with flour and leave to rise on floured baking parchment for about 20 minutes, until soft and puffy.

Meanwhile, toss the aubergine and garlic cloves with the olive oil in a roasting tin and roast for 20 minutes.

Lightly squeeze any excess moisture out of the mozzarella then cut it into cubes. Remove the roasting tin from the oven and cool for 10 minutes before stirring in the tomatoes, mozzarella and basil. Season to taste.

Roll or pull the risen balls of dough into 20-cm circles directly onto 2 sheets of non-stick baking parchment. Slide these onto 2 rimless baking sheets. Spread a quarter of the vegetable mixture on one half of each calzone, leaving just over 1 cm around the edge for sealing. Season well. Fold the uncovered half of the dough over the filling. Pinch and twist the edges firmly together so that the filling doesn't escape during cooking. Brush with olive oil and sprinkle with Parmesan.

Working quickly, open the oven door and slide paper and calzone onto the hot baking sheets. Bake for 30 minutes, swapping the baking sheets around halfway or until the crust is puffed up and golden. Remove from the oven and leave to stand for 2–3 minutes before serving (this will allow the filling to cool slightly). Serve hot or warm.

In Naples, this is known as 'filled pizza' or *pizza ripieno*, but the word 'calzone' literally means 'trouser leg' as it was thought the shape was reminiscent of the traditional everyday dress of the street – a sort of tapered pantaloon.

potato and mozzarella calzone
calzone di patate e mozzarella

½ recipe Basic Pizza Dough (page 12), making just 1 ball of dough

50–75 g buffalo mozzarella or cow's milk mozzarella (*fior di latte*)

200 g potatoes, peeled and very thinly sliced

2 tablespoons extra virgin olive oil, plus extra to glaze

1 garlic clove, finely chopped

1 tablespoon chopped fresh rosemary

sea salt and freshly ground black pepper

a *testo*, terracotta bakestone or a large, heavy baking sheet

a pizza peel or rimless baking sheet

Makes 1 calzone, 25–35 cm

Put the testo, terracotta bakestone or a large, heavy baking sheet on the lower shelf of the oven. Preheat the oven to 220°C (425°F) Gas 7 for at least 30 minutes.

Lightly squeeze any excess moisture out of the mozzarella then cut it into cubes. Toss the sliced potato with the olive oil, garlic and rosemary, then add the mozzarella.

Uncover the dough, punch out the air and roll or pull into a 25-cm circle directly onto non-stick baking parchment. Slide this onto the pizza peel or rimless baking sheet. Spread one half of the calzone with the potato mixture, leaving just over 1 cm around the edge for sealing. Season well. Fold the uncovered half of the dough over the filling. Pinch and twist the edges firmly together so that the filling doesn't escape during cooking.

Working quickly, open the oven door and slide paper and calzone onto the hot bakestone or baking sheet. If you are brave, try to shoot the calzone into the oven so that it leaves the paper behind – this takes practice!

Bake for 10 minutes, then carefully slide out the baking parchment. Bake for a further 25–30 minutes or until the crust is puffed up and golden. Remove from the oven and brush with a little olive oil. Leave to stand for 2–3 minutes before serving (this will allow the filling to cool slightly). Serve hot or warm.

These little pies could be made into a traditional calzone by breaking a whole egg into the filling, but for a special occasion or a picnic, they look great cooked in bun tins.

egg and spinach pizza pies
torte al spinaci, ricotta e uove

1 recipe Basic Pizza Dough (page 12) or Sicilian Pizza Dough (page 14)

2 tablespoons extra virgin olive oil, plus extra to glaze

1 small onion, finely chopped

250 g fresh spinach, washed

250 g ricotta

4 tablespoons freshly grated Parmesan cheese

75 g rocket, finely chopped

1 teaspoon chopped fresh tarragon

freshly grated nutmeg

8 eggs

sea salt and freshly ground black pepper

a testo, terracotta bakestone or a large, heavy baking sheet

two 4-hole bun/muffin tins

Makes 8 pizza pies

Place the testo, terracotta bakestone or a large, heavy baking sheet on the lower shelf of the oven. Preheat the oven to 220°C (425°F) Gas 7 for at least 30 minutes.

Heat the olive oil in a frying pan, add the onion and fry for 5 minutes until golden. Leave to cool. Steam the spinach until just wilted, refresh in cold water, then squeeze out as much moisture as possible and roughly chop. Beat the spinach and onions into the ricotta with the Parmesan, rocket and tarragon. Season well with salt, pepper and nutmeg.

Uncover the dough, punch out the air then tip out onto a floured surface. Roll or pull to a thin disc. Cut out 8 circles roughly 16 cm in diameter. Use these to line each bun/muffin cup. Fill each pie with some of the ricotta mixture. Make a small indent in each filling. Break the eggs one at a time, separating the yolks from the whites. Slip a yolk into the indent of each pie. Season. Roll the pastry offcuts into long, thin ropes and cut into 16 lengths. Use these to make a cross on top of each pie, sealing the edges with a little water. Brush lightly with olive oil.

Bake in the oven for 10 minutes until the egg is just set and the dough cooked. Eat hot.

I have never quite worked out why these little filled and rolled pizzas are called *stromboli*. Stromboli is a live volcano and one of the Aeolian islands off the coast of northern Sicily. Maybe it describes the eruption of flavours and filling when the pizzas are cut open, or the black and red colours of the filling. These are better eaten at room temperature and are perfect for picnics and packed lunches. Meat-eaters can cover the red pepper with slices of cooked ham before rolling up.

stromboli

1 recipe Basic Pizza Dough (page 12) or Sicilian Pizza Dough (page 14)

8 tablespoons Fiery Red Pesto (page 20)

4 large red peppers

4 tablespoons olive oil

125 g black olives, stoned and chopped

a large baking sheet, lined with parchment paper

Makes 4 stromboli

Preheat the oven to 200°C (400°F) Gas 6.

Rub the peppers with the olive oil and roast in the oven for 25–30 minutes until charred on the outside. Peel the peppers, pull them apart and remove the seeds and stalks. Leave to cool.

Meanwhile, uncover the dough, punch out the air and knead 55 g of the olives into it. Divide the dough into 4. Roll each piece into a rectangle about 17 x 24 cm. Spread pesto over each one, sprinkle the remaining chopped olives over the top, and cover with the peppers, leaving a 1-cm rim around the edges of the dough. Roll up from the shorter side. Make sure the seam is underneath the pizza. Pinch the open ends to seal, and tuck them under. Squash the rolled pizzas slightly – they should now look a little like French pains au chocolat. Arrange them well apart on the prepared baking sheet, cover with lightly oiled clingfilm and leave to rise for 20 minutes.

Remove the clingfilm and bake the stromboli for 25–30 minutes until risen and golden. Leave to cool for 5 minutes before cutting open and serving, or leave to cool completely.

At one time, this pie was made with sweet pastry but nowadays it is made with pizza dough. You can use any filling you like, but ricotta and pockets of melting mozzarella are essential. It is very rich and filling, and equally good eaten at room temperature.

rustic country pie
torta rustica

1 recipe Basic Pizza Dough (page 12)

5 eggs, separated

300 g ricotta, sieved

100 g cow's milk mozzarella (*fior di latte*), diced

100 g smoked mozzarella, diced

55 g Speck ham, chopped

55 g salami, chopped

4 tablespoons freshly grated Parmesan cheese

10 cherry tomatoes, halved

sea salt and freshly ground black pepper

a pizza pan or springform cake tin, 25 x 4 cm, lightly oiled

Makes 1 pie, 25 cm

Place a baking sheet in the middle of the oven. Preheat the oven to 180°C (350°F) Gas 4.

Beat 4 of the egg yolks together, then beat into the ricotta with plenty of salt and pepper. Whisk all the egg whites until stiff and fold into the ricotta mixture. Now fold in both types of mozzarella, the Speck and salami, and finally the Parmesan.

Uncover the dough, punch out the air and roll or pull two-thirds of it into a 35-cm circle. Use this to line the pizza pan, draping the extra dough over the edge. Spoon in the filling and smooth out the surface. Roll out the remaining dough thinly on a floured surface. Cut it into narrow strips and use them to make a lattice over the top of the pie. Secure the ends to the edge of the pastry with a little water. Trim around the edge with a sharp knife. Place a halved cherry tomato in each square of the lattice and season again. Beat the remaining egg yolk with a pinch of salt and brush the edges of the pie with it.

Bake in the oven for 40–45 minutes until golden. Remove from the oven and leave to stand for 10 minutes before serving.

This magnificent double-crust pie is filled with Sicilian bounty – aubergines, tomatoes, tuna and basil. The breadcrumbs between the layers soak up the juices and keep the filling firm but moist. I have even made this with fresh, boned sardines instead of tuna. Out of season, tinned tuna in oil works very well.

aubergine and tuna double-crust pizza
scacciata

1 recipe Sicilian Pizza Dough (page 14)

4 tablespoons Classic Pesto Genovese (page 19)

4 tablespoons extra virgin olive oil, plus extra to glaze

2 aubergines, thinly sliced

55 g dried breadcrumbs

55 g freshly grated pecorino cheese

two 150-g fresh tuna steaks, sliced horizontally

4 tomatoes, thinly sliced

sea salt and freshly ground black pepper

a testo, terracotta bakestone or a large, heavy baking sheet

a pizza pan or springform cake tin, 25 x 4 cm, lightly oiled

Makes 1 pie, 25 cm

Put the testo, terracotta bakestone or a large, heavy baking sheet on the lower shelf of the oven. Preheat the oven to 220°C (425°F) Gas 7 for at least 30 minutes.

Heat the olive oil in a frying pan and fry the aubergines until golden brown. Drain on kitchen paper. Mix the breadcrumbs with the pecorino.

Uncover the dough, punch out the air and roll or pull two-thirds of it into a 35-cm circle. Use this to line the pizza pan, draping the extra dough over the edge. Arrange the aubergine slices over the base and sprinkle with a quarter of the breadcrumb mixture. Arrange the tuna slices on top of this and spread over the pesto. Sprinkle with another quarter of the breadcrumb mixture. Arrange the tomatoes over the tuna and pesto, season and sprinkle with another quarter of the breadcrumb mixture.

Roll or pull the remaining dough into a 27-cm circle. Brush the edge of the dough with a little water. Lay the circle of dough over the pie and press the edges to seal. Trim off the excess dough with a sharp knife. Brush the top with olive oil and sprinkle with the remaining breadcrumb mixture. Make 2 slashes in the centre of the pie. Bake in the oven for 35–45 minutes until golden. Serve warm or cold.

This double-crust pizza was made famous by the nuns of San Vito lo Capo in Sicily. My version contains ricotta and is a true meat feast. I regularly make it when I am teaching in Sicily. We have a special pizza day when we make doughs and toppings then head for the farmhouse with its antique bread oven. This is the first pizza we make and we waste no time tucking into it.

Italian sausage, potato and ricotta double-crust sfinciune
sfinciune al salsicce e patate

1 recipe Sicilian Pizza Dough (page 14)

2 tablespoons extra virgin olive oil, plus extra to glaze

200 g potatoes, peeled and finely diced

2 onions, finely chopped

1 teaspoon dried oregano

250 g fresh Italian sausage, skinned

1 teaspoon fennel seeds

2 tablespoons chopped fresh sage

125 g ricotta

sea salt and freshly ground black pepper

a testo, terracotta bakestone or a large, heavy baking sheet

a rimless baking sheet

Makes 1 double-crust pizza, 30 cm

Place the testo, terracotta bakestone or a large, heavy baking sheet on the lower shelf of the oven. Preheat the oven to 220°C (425°F) Gas 7 for at least 30 minutes.

Heat the oil in a frying pan and add the potatoes and onions. Cook for 5–10 minutes until the onion starts to colour and the potato is soft. Stir in the oregano. Season, then transfer to a bowl to cool. Fry the sausage briefly in the same frying pan, breaking it up with the back of a fork. Add the fennel seeds and sage and fry for a couple of minutes – but not too long or the meat will toughen. Season well, then leave to cool.

Uncover the dough, knock out the air and divide into 2. Roll each piece into a thin, 30-cm circle directly onto baking parchment. Spread the potato and onion mixture onto one circle, leaving a 1-cm rim around the edge. Dot with the sausage and the cheese. Season. Brush the edge with water and lay the remaining circle on top. Pinch and roll the edges to seal. Brush with a little olive oil. Make 2 slashes in the centre of the pie, then slide onto the rimless baking sheet.

Working quickly, open the oven door and slide paper and pizza onto the hot bakestone or baking sheet. If you are brave, try to shoot the pizza into the oven so that it leaves the paper behind – this takes practice!

Bake for 10 minutes, then carefully slide out the baking parchment. Bake the pizza for a further 25–30 minutes, or until the crust is puffed up and golden. Remove from the oven and brush with a little olive oil. Leave to stand for 5 minutes before serving. Eat hot, warm or cold.

This is almost an Italian equivalent of hot garlic bread, but much better. You can use ordinary pizza dough, or enrich it with egg. The thin dough base is smothered in pesto and green olives, rolled up to look like a long Swiss roll and left to rise again. Drenched in garlic oil and smothered in pecorino, the smell alone wafting from the oven is to die for!

rolled pesto, olive and garlic bread
rotolo di pane con olive, aglio e basilico

1 recipe Classic Pesto Genovese (page 19)

500 g Italian '00' flour or plain white flour

1 teaspoon sugar

½ teaspoon fine sea salt

25 g fresh yeast, 1 tablespoon dried active yeast or 2 teaspoons fast-action dried yeast

1 egg, beaten

3 tablespoons extra virgin olive oil

350 ml hand-hot water

200 g large green olives, stoned and roughly chopped

200 g freshly grated pecorino or Parmesan cheese

2–3 tablespoons garlic-infused olive oil

sea salt and freshly ground black pepper

a pizza peel or rimless baking sheet

a terracotta bakestone or a large, heavy baking sheet

Serves 6 as a loaf

Sift the flour, sugar and salt into a large bowl and make a well in the centre. Crumble in the fresh yeast or sprinkle in the dried yeast, if using. If you are using dried active yeast, follow the manufacturer's instructions. Rub in the yeast until the mixture resembles fine breadcrumbs. Pour in the beaten egg, olive oil and the hand-hot water and mix until the dough comes together. Knead the dough energetically, on a floured surface, for 5 minutes until soft, smooth and elastic. Put it in a lightly oiled bowl, cover with clingfilm or a damp tea towel and leave to rise in a warm place until doubled in size – about 1½ hours.

Preheat the oven to 200°C (400°F) Gas 6.

When risen, knock back the dough, then roll or pull into a large rectangle as thinly as you can, directly onto a sheet of non-stick baking parchment. Spread the dough liberally with the pesto, leaving a 1-cm rim all around the dough, then scatter over the olives and 125 g of the pecorino. Season. Using the parchment paper, roll the dough up like a Swiss roll, starting from the long side. Slide the dough onto another sheet of parchment making sure the seam is underneath. Brush with the garlic oil and sprinkle with the remaining pecorino.

Slide the rolled bread onto the pizza peel or rimless baking sheet. Working quickly, open the oven door and slide paper and bread onto the hot bakestone or baking sheet.

Bake for 20 minutes, then carefully slide out the baking parchment. Bake for a further 5 minutes until the crust is golden and the cheese melted but still white. Remove from the oven and serve warm (not hot) or cold in slices.

These are delicious little savoury rolls made just like Chelsea buns and baked together in a tin. Take the whole lot to the dinner table and break off your own little roll. Perfect with drinks on a hot summer night, or instead of bread, they disappear very fast!

walnut and parsley rolls
sfogliate ai noci e prezzemolo

1 recipe Basic Pizza Dough (page 12)

200 g walnut pieces

30 g fresh parsley leaves

2 garlic cloves

100 ml extra virgin olive oil

sea salt and freshly ground black pepper

a deep pizza pan or springform cake tin, 23 cm, lightly oiled

Makes about 20 small rolls

Preheat the oven to 200°C (400°F) Gas 6.

Put the walnuts, parsley and garlic in a food processor and process until evenly chopped. While the machine is running, pour in the olive oil. Season to taste.

Uncover the dough, punch out the air and roll or pull into a rectangle, 60 x 20 cm, directly onto a large sheet of non-stick baking parchment.

Spread the walnut mixture over the dough. Season. Using the parchment paper, roll the dough up like a Swiss roll, starting from the long side. Slide the dough onto another sheet of parchment making sure the seam is underneath. Using a large and very sharp knife cut the roll into 20 even pieces. Cut the dough quickly and smoothly each time – don't saw it or it will stick! Arrange the rolls cut-side up in the prepared pizza pan, spacing them close together but not quite touching. Cover with oiled clingfilm or a damp tea towel and leave to rise to the top of the pan for about 30 minutes.

Remove the clingfilm and bake the rolls for 35–45 minutes or until golden. Leave to cool in the pan if you want them very soft, or turn them out onto a rack to cool if you'd like them drier. Serve warm.

We all love bread dough, but often the dough balls in pizza restaurants are just too heavy. This is my version – little balls of pizza dough washed with a salty glaze. Split them while they are still hot, pull out the doughy centre and fill with cool, creamy ricotta, a spoonful of aubergine antipasto and some good tinned tuna in oil.

dough balls
panizze

1 recipe Basic Pizza Dough (page 12) or Sicilian Pizza Dough (page 14)

1 tablespoon fine sea salt

ricotta, marinated aubergine and tinned tuna, to serve

a large baking sheet lined with parchment paper

Makes 10–12 balls

Preheat the oven to 200°C (400°F) Gas 6.

Uncover the dough, punch out the air and divide it into 12. Shape each piece into a neat ball.

Put the dough balls on the prepared baking sheet, spacing them well apart. Cover loosely with lightly oiled clingfilm or a damp tea towel and leave to rise again until doubled in size – about 30 minutes.

Dissolve the salt in 3 tablespoons water. When the dough balls have risen, brush them with the salt solution.

Bake the rolls for 15–20 minutes until risen and browned. Cool on a wire rack then split and fill with the ricotta, aubergine and tuna.

This is a revelation! If you like baking, then try these – they are very easy to make, versatile (make them any shape or size you like), and the result is so professional. Indeed, they are becoming a very popular snack. Once baked, they can be frozen and reheated, as long as they are wrapped in aluminium foil to keep them moist. They must be warm when they are split or they will crack.

pizza pockets
pagnotielli

½ recipe Basic Pizza Dough (page 12), making just 1 ball of dough

a terracotta bakestone or a large, heavy baking sheet

Makes 4–6 pizza pockets, depending on size

Place the testo, terracotta bakestone or a large heavy baking sheet on the lower shelf of the oven. Preheat the oven to 220°C (425°F) Gas 7 for at least 30 minutes.

Uncover the dough, punch out the air and divide it into 6 (or however many you wish). Shape each piece into a round ball then roll out to an oval. Using a fork with large tines, prick them all over (but not too much).

Lay the pizza pockets on 2 sheets of lightly floured baking parchment. If they don't all fit, bake them in batches.

Working quickly, open the oven door and slide the paper onto the hot bakestone or baking sheet.

Bake for 3–5 minutes, until very puffed up and very pale golden. Remove from the oven and wrap in a clean tea towel to keep warm and soft if you need to cook another batch.

When they are all cooked, quickly cut them in half across the middle and open out the pocket. Stuff with your chosen filling, for example cooked ham, tomato and mozzarella. Wrap loosely in aluminium foil, then return to the oven for 2 minutes. Unwrap, add salad leaves and eat immediately.

focaccia

The word *focaccia* means a bread baked directly on the hearth, and derives from the Latin word for 'hearth' (*focus*). In Ligurian dialect focaccia is known as *fugassa* from which the French word *fougasse* originates. Although a rustic focaccia can be made with any basic pizza dough, the secret of a truly light, thick focaccia lies in giving the dough three risings, and dimpling the dough so that it traps olive oil while it bakes. Follow the instructions on page 15 for shaping the bread.

deep-pan focaccia

750 g Italian '00' flour or plain white flour, plus extra as necessary

½ teaspoon fine sea salt

25 g fresh yeast, 1 tablespoon dried active yeast or 2 teaspoons fast-action dried yeast

150 ml extra virgin olive oil

400–450 ml hand-hot water

coarse sea salt or rock salt

fresh rosemary sprigs (optional)

2 cake tins, pie or pizza pans, 25 x 4 cm, lightly oiled

Makes 2 focaccias, 25 cm

Sift the flour and fine sea salt into a large bowl and make a well in the centre. Crumble in the fresh yeast, or add dried yeast, if using. If you are using dried active yeast, follow the manufacturer's instructions. Pour in 50 ml of the olive oil, then rub in the yeast until the mixture resembles fine breadcrumbs. Pour in the hand-hot water and mix together with your hands until the dough comes together.

Tip the dough out onto a floured surface, wash and dry your hands and knead energetically for 10 minutes until smooth and elastic. The dough should be very soft (almost too soft to handle), but don't worry about it too much at this stage.

Put the dough in a lightly oiled bowl, cover with clingfilm or a damp tea towel and leave to rise in a warm place until doubled in size – about 1½ hours.

Uncover the dough, punch out the air and divide into 2. Shape each piece into a round ball on a lightly floured surface and roll out into two 25-cm circles and place in the tins. Cover with clingfilm or a damp tea towel and leave to rise for 30 minutes.

Preheat the oven to 200°C (400°F) Gas 6.

Follow the instructions on page 15 for shaping your bread.

Spray the focaccias with water and bake for 20–25 minutes until risen and golden. Drizzle with the remaining olive oil then transfer to a wire rack to cool. Eat on the same day or leave to cool, then wrap up and freeze. When you remove the focaccia from the freezer, thaw and wrap in aluminium foil, then reheat for 5 minutes in a hot oven.

This is a wonderful example of the traditional focaccia, as it is baked directly on the bakestone or on a hot baking sheet. If the base is floured very well the focaccia can be slipped directly onto the stone or baking sheet, leaving the parchment paper behind. This is the kind of focaccia that you tear and dip into yet more fruity olive oil.

thin focaccia

1 recipe Deep-pan Focaccia (page 86), risen twice but uncooked

100 ml extra virgin olive oil

coarse sea salt or rock salt

2 testi, terracotta bakestones or large, heavy baking sheets

a rimless baking sheet, lined with parchment paper

Makes 2 large, flat focaccias

Put the 2 testi, terracotta bakestones or large, heavy baking sheets on the lower shelf of the oven. Preheat the oven to 220°C (425°F) Gas 7 for at least 30 minutes.

Uncover the dough, punch out the air and divide into 2. Shape each piece into a rough ball then pull and stretch the dough to a large oval shape – as large as will fit in your oven. Place on the rimless baking sheet. Cover with lightly oiled clingfilm or a damp tea towel and leave to rise for 30 minutes.

Remove the clingfilm and, using your fingertips, make deep dimples all over the surface of the dough right down to the baking sheet. Drizzle over all but 2 tablespoons of the remaining oil. Spray the focaccias with water and sprinkle generously with salt. Working quickly, open the oven door and slide paper and focaccia onto the hot bakestones or baking sheet.

Bake for 15 minutes, then carefully slide out the baking parchment. Bake the focaccia for a further 15 minutes, or until the crust is golden. Brush or drizzle with the remaining olive oil then transfer to a wire rack to cool. Eat on the same day or leave to cool, then wrap up and freeze. When you remove it from the freezer, thaw and wrap in aluminium foil, then reheat for 5 minutes in a hot oven.

This is just the thing to make when there are very good fresh figs around – you will be very popular, as this is just heavenly! The combination of sweet juicy figs, salty ham and rich, runny Taleggio is heady stuff. Mozzarella and Gorgonzola would both work well here (you need a soft melting cheese) and I've even made it using over-ripe peaches instead of figs.

stuffed focaccia with figs, prosciutto and Taleggio
focaccia farcita

½ recipe Deep-pan Focaccia (page 86), making just 1 focaccia

3 tablespoons extra virgin olive oil

6 fresh ripe figs, quartered or sliced

6 slices prosciutto crudo

125 g Taleggio or Gorgonzola cheese, sliced

sea salt and freshly ground black pepper

Makes 1 focaccia, 25 cm

Bake the focaccia without the rosemary following the recipe on page 86. Remove from the oven and tip out of the tin.

Holding the hot focaccia in a tea towel to protect your hands, slice through it horizontally with a serrated knife.

Brush the insides with the olive oil. Fill with the figs, prosciutto and Taleggio, seasoning as you go. Put the top back on and wrap loosely in aluminium foil, then return to the hot oven for 5 minutes. Unwrap, cut into thick wedges and eat whilst warm and melting.

This is a good focaccia for making outrageous sandwiches or serving in thick slices smothered in fresh ricotta. Replacing some of the liquid in the dough with tomato purée (or even all the water with tomato juice) gives it a beautiful, rusty red colour, studded with bright red pepper and dark chunks of salami or chorizo.

fiery focaccia
focaccia alla diavola

½ recipe Deep-pan Focaccia (page 86), making the changes stated in this recipe

4 tablespoons tomato purée

4–6 red chillies or Peppadews, diced

2 red peppers, roasted, deseeded and diced

100 g *salame piccante* or chorizo, cubed

75 g *provolone piccante*, Emmental or Gruyère cheese, cubed

100 ml extra virgin olive oil, plus extra to glaze

coarse sea salt or rock salt

a cake tin or pizza pan, 25 x 4 cm, lightly oiled

Makes 1 focaccia, 25 cm

Make the focaccia dough following the recipe on page 86, but using 4 tablespoons tomato purée dissolved in the water. Knead the dough and give it the first rising.

Uncover the dough, punch out the air and pull or roll it out into a rough circle. Dot with the chillies, red peppers, salami, provolone and lots of freshly ground black pepper. Flip one half of the dough over and lightly knead to incorporate the ingredients. Shape into a rough ball on a lightly floured surface and pat into the prepared tin. Cover lightly with clingfilm or a damp tea towel and leave to rise for 30 minutes.

Remove the clingfilm and, using your fingertips, make deep dimples all over the surface of the dough. Drizzle over the olive oil, re-cover very lightly with clingfilm and leave to rise for a final 30 minutes until very puffy.

Preheat the oven to 200°C (400°F) Gas 6.

Uncover the focaccia, mist with water and sprinkle generously with salt. Bake for 20–25 minutes until risen and golden. Transfer to a wire rack, brush with olive oil and leave to cool. Eat on the same day or leave to cool, then wrap up and freeze. When you remove it from the freezer, thaw and wrap in aluminium foil, then reheat for 5 minutes in a hot oven.

This is an unusual bread from the coastal areas of Lunigiana and made from a mixture of cornmeal and wheat flour. It is traditionally made between November and the end of January to coincide with the olive harvest. It is cooked in a wood-fired oven on a bed of chestnut leaves, and takes on a deep brown crust. It must be eaten on the day, and is often served as part of an antipasto.

cornmeal and olive focaccia with rosemary and sage
la marocca

500 g Italian '00' flour

300 g fine polenta flour (*farina gialla* or *granoturco*)

two 7-g sachets fast-action dried yeast

200 g black olives, stoned and halved

3 tablespoons pine nuts

2 tablespoons chopped fresh sage

2 tablespoons chopped fresh rosemary

2–3 garlic cloves, finely chopped

3 tablespoons extra virgin olive oil, plus extra to drizzle

450 ml hand-hot water

rock salt and freshly ground black pepper

a Swiss roll tin, 33 x 23 cm, oiled

Makes 1 focaccia, 33 x 23 cm

Mix the flours and yeast in a large bowl. Add the olives, pine nuts, sage, rosemary and garlic, then mix. Make a well in the centre and add the olive oil mixed with the hand-hot water. Mix to a very soft dough, turn out onto a lightly floured work surface and knead very vigorously for 10 minutes.

Roll or pull the dough into a rectangle to fit the Swiss roll tin, pushing the dough into the corners. Cover with clingfilm or a damp tea towel and leave to rise in a warm place for about 20–30 minutes until quite puffy.

Meanwhile, preheat the oven to 200°C (400°F) Gas 6.

Using your fingertips, make deep dimples all over the dough and drizzle with olive oil. Sprinkle with salt and bake for about 35 minutes, until risen, firm and dark golden.

Now here's something to start the day properly. Little warm focaccias are split, the insides brushed with a few drops of truffle oil mixed with melted butter, and filled with crispy fried pancetta and a fried egg. A real special-occasion dish. Be careful when you use truffle oil, as it can be overpowering; and be sure to use real truffle-infused oil not the artificially flavoured variety.

truffled breakfast focaccia
focaccia tartufata con pancetta

½ recipe Deep-pan Focaccia (page 86), making just 1 ball of dough, up to the first rising

4 tablespoons extra virgin olive oil, plus extra to fry

a few drops of good truffle oil

100 g unsalted butter, melted

12 thin rashers pancetta or streaky bacon

4 eggs

sea salt and freshly ground black pepper

4 deep, springform cake tins, 12 cm each, lightly oiled

Makes 4 focaccias, 12 cm

Uncover the dough, punch out the air and divide into 4. Shape each piece into a round ball on a lightly floured surface. Roll out into 12-cm circles and place in the prepared cake tins. Cover with clingfilm or a damp tea towel and leave to rise for 30 minutes.

Preheat the oven to 200°C (400°F) Gas 6.

Using your fingertips, make deep dimples all over the dough right to the base of the tins and drizzle with the olive oil. Re-cover and leave to rise to the top of the tins – about 30 minutes.

Spray the focaccias with water, sprinkle generously with salt and bake for 20–25 minutes until risen and golden.

While the focaccias are baking, mix the truffle oil with the melted butter and keep warm. Grill the pancetta until crisp – or bake in the oven at the same time as the focaccia. Fry the eggs in olive oil and keep warm.

When the focaccias are ready, tip them out of their tins, hold them in a tea towel to protect your hands and slice through them horizontally with a serrated knife. (If they seem too thick, shave a slice off the inside.) Brush the insides with the truffle butter and lay three pancetta rashers and an egg on each one. Replace the tops and serve immediately.

To make the focaccias ahead of time, bake them and leave to cool, then wrap up and freeze. When you remove them from the freezer, thaw and wrap in aluminium foil, then reheat for 5 minutes in a hot oven.

Making a bread by mixing mashed potato with flour and anointing it lavishly with good olive oil is common all over Italy, especially in Liguria and Puglia, where some of the best olive oil comes from. Sometimes, the top is covered in paper thin slices of potato and scattered with rosemary before baking. Either way it is delicious, but quite dense. I tend not to stone the olives for this as they can dry out too much in the oven.

potato and olive focaccia

500 g floury potatoes (such as King Edwards, Golden Wonder or Kerr's Pinks), unpeeled

600 g Italian '00' flour or plain white flour, plus extra as necessary

½ teaspoon fine sea salt

25 g fresh yeast, 1 tablespoon dried active yeast or 2 teaspoons fast-action dried yeast

200 g large, juicy green olives, stones in

150 ml extra virgin olive oil

sea salt or rock salt

two cake tins, 25 x 4 cm, or a large rectangular tin, lightly oiled

Makes two focaccias, 25 cm

Boil or bake the potatoes in their skins and peel them whilst still warm. Mash them or pass them through a potato ricer.

Sift the flour with the fine salt into a large bowl and make a well in the centre. Crumble in the fresh yeast, or add dried yeast, if using. If you are using dried active yeast, follow the manufacturer's instructions. Add the potatoes and mix together with your hands until the dough comes together. Tip the dough out onto a floured surface, wash and dry your hands and knead energetically for 10 minutes until smooth and elastic. The dough should be soft; if it isn't, add a couple of tablespoons warm water.

Divide the dough into 2, shape each piece into a round ball on a lightly floured surface and roll out into two 25-cm circles or a large rectangle to fit whichever tin you are using. Put the dough in the tin, cover with clingfilm or a damp tea towel and leave to rise for 2 hours.

Preheat the oven to 200°C (400°F) Gas 6.

Uncover the dough, scatter over the olives, and, using your fingertips, make deep dimples all over the surface of the dough, pushing in some of the olives here and there. Drizzle with 100 ml of the olive oil, re-cover and leave to rise for another 30 minutes.

Uncover the dough, spray with water and sprinkle generously with salt. Bake for 20–25 minutes until risen and golden brown. Brush or drizzle with the remaining olive oil then transfer to a wire rack to cool. Eat on the same day, or leave to cool, then wrap up and freeze. When you remove the focaccia from the freezer, thaw and wrap in aluminium foil, then reheat for 5 minutes in a hot oven.

When I was teaching in Italy, I made focaccia in all shapes and sizes, and with many different flours. I wondered how it would taste if I incorporated my native oatmeal. I decided to use fine oatmeal and '00' flour and to scatter porridge oats and salt on top. The result was a thin, crisp, but still moist focaccia, with a golden, crunchy topping. Make sure all the ingredients are at warm room temperature, and if necessary, warm them in a low oven – this will help the dough to rise.

oatmeal focaccia
focaccia al avena

2½ teaspoons dried active yeast

1 teaspoon sugar

350–450 ml hand-hot water

125 g fine oatmeal, warmed

500 g Italian '00' flour or plain unbleached white flour, warmed

2 teaspoons English mustard powder

1 teaspoon freshly ground black pepper

2 teaspoons fine salt

2 tablespoons extra virgin olive oil, plus extra to drizzle

3–4 tablespoons porridge oats

rock salt

two Swiss roll tins, 23 x 32 cm, oiled

Makes 2 thin, rectangular focaccias

Whisk the yeast and sugar into the hand-hot water and stir in the warmed oatmeal. Cover and leave to stand in a warm place for 10–15 minutes until frothy.

Sift the flour, mustard powder, pepper and salt into a warm bowl, pour in the oatmeal mixture and add the olive oil. Mix to a soft dough. Add a little extra warm water if the dough looks too dry. Turn out and knead for at least 10 minutes or until elastic (see page 10).

Place in a lightly oiled bowl, cover with clingfilm or a damp tea towel and leave to rise in a warm place for about 1 hour or until doubled in size.

Uncover the dough, punch out the air and divide in 2. Pull and roll each piece to fit the Swiss roll tins. Place in the tins and press into the corners. Prick the dough all over with a fork and scatter the oatmeal flakes and salt over the top. Cover with oiled clingfilm or a damp tea towel and leave to rise until puffy – 30–60 minutes.

Preheat the oven to 200°C (400°F) Gas 6.

Drizzle the focaccias with olive oil and bake for 25 minutes until golden. Remove from the oven and drizzle with a little more olive oil. Cool on a wire rack and serve cut into thin fingers. Best eaten the same day.

Doesn't focaccia *have* to have dimples? Well, in general it does but it varies depending on where you live in Italy. This recipe merits being a focaccia because it is made with an olive-oil enriched dough, and it has a filling, like so many focaccias. It's the Italian equivalent of bacon and egg pie but it's made with lots of parsley and lovely fresh ricotta.

ricotta and Parma ham focaccia
torta di focaccia con ricotta e prosciutto crudo

½ recipe Deep-pan Focaccia (page 86), making just 1 ball of dough, up to the first rising

4 eggs

100 g ricotta

6 tablespoons chopped fresh parsley or rocket

55 g freshly grated pecorino cheese

150 g thinly sliced Parma ham

extra virgin olive oil, to glaze

sea salt and freshly ground black pepper

a pizza pan or springform cake tin, 23 x 4 cm, lightly oiled

Makes 1 focaccia, 23 cm

Preheat the oven to 220°C (425°F) Gas 7 for at least 30 minutes.

While the dough rises, make the filling. Put the eggs, ricotta and parsley in a food processor and process until smooth. Pour into a jug and mix in the pecorino. Season with pepper but no salt.

Uncover the dough, punch out the air and knead until smooth. Roll two-thirds of it into a 32-cm circle and use this to line the pizza pan, draping the extra dough over the edge. Alternate layers of Parma ham and ricotta mixture until they are all used up.

Roll the remaining dough into a 27-cm circle. Brush the edge of the filled dough with water. Lift the circle of dough over the pie and press the edges to seal. Trim off the excess dough with a sharp knife. Brush with olive oil. Make 2 slashes in the centre of the pie. Bake for 20–25 minutes until golden. Serve warm or cold.

This amazing focaccia features the reverse of dimpling – cobbles, which ooze cheese when they are cut open. The pastry is made with olive oil and has no yeast in it. The secret is to roll out the pastry very thinly so that it cooks quickly and hasn't got time to absorb the melting cheese. The breadcrumbs are there to absorb any whey escaping from the cheese.

oozing cheese pizza
focaccia con formaggio

250 g Italian '00' flour

100 ml warm water

3 tablespoons extra virgin olive oil, plus extra to glaze

5 balls cow's milk mozzarella (*fior di latte*), or a smoked mozzarella, which will be firmer

6 tablespoons dried breadcrumbs

sea salt

a testo, terracotta bakestone or a large, heavy baking sheet

a rimless baking sheet

Makes 1 focaccia, 30 cm

First, make an unleavened dough by mixing the flour, the warm water and the olive oil. Add more warm water if necessary. Knead well until smooth and elastic, then place in a bowl, cover and leave to rest for 1 hour.

Put the testo, terracotta bakestone or a large, heavy baking sheet on the lower shelf of the oven. Preheat the oven to 220°C (425°F) Gas 7 for at least 30 minutes.

Divide the dough into 2, making one piece slightly larger than the other. Using plenty of flour for dusting, roll the larger piece as thinly as you can into a 30-cm circle directly onto non-stick baking parchment and slide onto a rimless baking sheet.

Cut the mozzarella balls in half and lightly squeeze out any moisture. Dip the bases in the dried breadcrumbs. Arrange the cheeses, domed-side up, over the pastry, adding any remaining breadcrumbs underneath each one. Roll out the remaining dough as thinly as you can and slightly larger than the base. Lift this over the cheeses and gently press the dough down and around each piece of cheese. The blunt edge of a biscuit cutter will help you to seal the edge of each mound – use a cutter that fits just around a mound. Make sure there are no holes for the cheese to run through. Twist and crimp the edges of the pizza together. Carefully brush with olive oil and sprinkle with salt.

Working quickly, open the oven door and slide paper and pizza onto the hot bakestone or baking sheet. If you are brave, try to shoot the pizza into the oven so that it leaves the paper behind – this takes practice!

Bake for 10–15 minutes or until golden, then remove from the oven and serve immediately, cut with a pizza wheel into oozing wedges.

This unusual cheese loaf is baked in a ring mould because the dough is made from a loose batter – almost a brioche – and the mould will hold it nicely. This sort of bread is normally only made for holidays and celebrations, but it's delicious toasted for breakfast; the smell will rouse even the sleepiest member of the household. The bread can easily be baked in a loaf tin but it is not quite as pretty.

Easter cheese focaccia
torta pasquale

25 g fresh yeast

200 ml hand-hot water

a pinch of sugar

4 eggs (at room temperature), beaten

500 g Italian '00' flour

100 g freshly grated Parmesan cheese

sea salt and freshly ground black pepper

relish or pesto, to serve

a ring mould, 23 cm, oiled and dusted with flour

Makes 1 ring, 23 cm

Dissolve the yeast in the hand-hot water with the sugar. Whisk in the eggs. Put the flour and Parmesan in an electric mixer and season. Pour in the yeast mixture and mix slowly, on a low setting, for 5 minutes until smooth. Turn up to medium and mix for a further 5 minutes. The batter should be very soft. Pour or scoop the batter into the prepared ring mould, cover with a damp tea towel and leave to rise for 1 hour or until puffy.

Preheat the oven to 180°C (350°F) Gas 4.

Bake the dough in the oven for 35–40 minutes until well risen and a deep, rich brown on top. Invert onto a wire rack and leave to stand for 10 minutes in the mould. Lift off the mould, turn the bread over and cool. Serve, in slices, with relish or pesto.

This is an unyeasted bread from Umbria, and very quick to rustle up. Little packets of baking powder are especially made for instant savoury doughs in Italy. When making this type of bread, work quickly, because as soon as the liquid comes into contact with the baking powder, a chemical reaction starts to aerate the bread. Use a light hand and get the dough into the oven as soon as possible.

Parmesan soda bread
torta reggiano

300 g Italian '00' flour

1 teaspoon baking powder

1 teaspoon salt

50 g freshly grated Parmesan cheese, plus extra to dust

50 g butter, melted and cooled

100–150 ml milk

2 medium eggs

a testo, terracotta bakestone or a large, heavy baking sheet

a rimless baking sheet, lined with non-stick baking parchment

Makes 1 loaf, approximately 23 cm

Put the testo, terracotta bakestone or a large, heavy baking sheet on the lower shelf of the oven. Preheat the oven to 190°C (375°F) Gas 5 for at least 30 minutes.

Sift the flour, baking powder and salt into a medium mixing bowl. Stir in the Parmesan and make a well in the centre.

Whisk the cooled, melted butter with 100 ml of the milk and the eggs, and pour into the well. Mix until *just* combined – overmixing will make the bread tough. The dough should be quite soft; if it isn't, add a little more milk. Turn out onto a floured work surface and knead briefly. Put the ball of dough directly onto a rimless baking sheet lined with non-stick baking parchment. Pat into a disc about 3 cm thick. Brush with a little extra milk, then mark into wedges with the back of a knife and dust with extra Parmesan.

Working quickly, open the oven door and slide paper and bread onto the hot bakestone or baking sheet. If you are brave, try to shoot the bread into the oven so that it leaves the paper behind – this takes practice!

Bake for 15 minutes, then carefully slide out the baking parchment. Bake for a further 5 minutes or until the crust is really golden. Remove from the oven and wrap in a tea towel. Serve warm, broken into wedges, ready to split and fill.

These little flatbreads are made with cornmeal and wheat flour. They are similar to English muffins and are served at local *sagre* (festivals) in the Lunigiana, Tuscany. Cooked on a girdle and ready in minutes, they are golden and puffy, and smell delicious. Fill them with cheese, meat or salami. You can use polenta for this, but whizz it with the flour in a food processor to refine it.

cornmeal muffins
focaccette di granoturco

25 g fresh yeast, 1 tablespoon dried active baking yeast or 2 teaspoons fast-action dried yeast

1 teaspoon sugar

400 ml hand-hot water

500 g Italian '00' flour

200 g fine cornmeal or polenta

1½ teaspoons fine sea salt

6 tablespoons extra virgin olive oil

a testo or heavy-based frying pan

Makes 8 muffins

In a medium bowl, cream the fresh yeast with the sugar and whisk in the hand-hot water. Leave for 10 minutes until frothy. For other yeasts, follow the manufacturer's instructions. Sift the flour, cornmeal and salt into a large bowl and make a well in the centre. Pour in the yeast mixture and the olive oil. Mix with a round-bladed knife, then your hands, until the dough comes together.

Tip out onto a lightly floured surface, wash and dry your hands (this will stop the dough sticking to them) then knead briskly for 5–10 minutes until smooth, shiny and elastic. (5 minutes for warm hands, 10 minutes for cold hands!) Try not to add any extra flour at this stage – a wetter dough is better. If you feel the dough is sticky, flour your hands and not the dough. The dough should be quite soft. If it is *really* too soft to handle, knead in a little more flour.

To test if the dough is ready, roll it into a fat sausage, take each end in either hand, lift the dough up and pull and stretch the dough outwards, gently wiggling it up and down – it should stretch out quite easily. If it doesn't, it needs more kneading.

Shape into a neat ball. Place in an oiled bowl, cover with clingfilm or a damp tea towel and leave to rise in a warm, draught-free place until doubled in size – about 1½ hours. Heat the testo or heavy-based frying pan on the hob until medium hot.

Uncover the dough, punch out the air, then tip out onto a lightly floured surface. Divide into 8 smooth balls, then flatten each into a disc about 1 cm thick. Slide 2 or 3 discs onto the hot testo or frying pan and cook for about 2 minutes on each side, until risen and deep brown on the underside.

Keep the cooked muffins warm and soft in a cloth or loosely wrapped in aluminium foil in a warm oven while cooking the rest. They are best served warm. Serve split and filled with cheese, alongside a selection of cold meats and salami.

Mixing wheat flour with chestnut flour gives this focaccia a wonderful sweet and savoury flavour – almost smoky. It is generally made during the autumn or winter months when chestnut flour is readily available and at its best. I serve it with lovely runny Gorgonzola and fresh pears as a dessert – with extra Vin Santo, of course.

chestnut and Vin Santo focaccia
focaccia di castagne e Vin Santo

500 g Italian '00' flour or plain white flour

200 g chestnut flour (*farina di castagne*)

1 teaspoon fine sea salt

25 g fresh yeast, 1 tablespoon dried active yeast or 2 teaspoons fast-action dried yeast

150 ml extra virgin olive oil

150 ml Vin Santo mixed with 300 ml water, warmed

rock salt, to sprinkle

2 cake tins, pie or pizza pans, 25 x 4 cm, lightly oiled

Makes 2 focaccias, 25 cm

Sift the flours and salt into a large bowl and make a well in the centre. Crumble in the fresh yeast. For other yeasts, follow the manufacturer's instructions.

Pour in 3 tablespoons of the olive oil, then rub into the yeast until the mixture resembles fine breadcrumbs. Pour the Vin Santo and water into the well and mix together until the dough comes together.

Tip out onto a lightly floured surface, wash and dry your hands (this will stop the dough sticking to them), then knead briskly for 10 minutes until smooth and elastic. The dough should be very soft, almost too soft to handle, but don't worry at this stage. Put in a lightly oiled bowl, cover with clingfilm or a damp tea towel and leave to rise in a warm place until doubled – about 1½ hours.

Uncover the dough, punch out the air, then divide into 2. Shape each piece into a round ball on a lightly floured surface. Roll out into 25-cm circles and put in the tins. Cover with clingfilm or a damp tea towel and leave to rise in a warm place for about 45 minutes or until very puffy and almost risen to the top of the tin.

Uncover the dough and, using your fingertips, make deep dimples all over the surface of the dough right to the base of the tin. Drizzle over the remaining oil, re-cover and leave to rise for a final 30 minutes.

Preheat the oven to 200°C (400°F) Gas 6.

Spray the focaccias with water, lightly sprinkle with rock salt and bake for 20–25 minutes until risen and golden. Transfer to a wire rack to cool. Eat on the same day or leave to cool, then wrap up and freeze. When you remove them from the freezer, thaw and wrap in aluminium foil, then reheat for 5 minutes in a hot oven.

The word *schiacciata* literally means 'flattened'. *Schiacciata con l'uva* is a puffy flatbread baked with the Chianti grape (Sangiovese) and sugar, and is only seen in bakers' shops at grape harvest time. My sweeter, richer version features black table grapes, walnuts, butter and brown sugar. Instead of grapes, you could use cherries, pine nuts or blueberries, or even raisins soaked overnight in Vin Santo or sherry.

sticky grape schiacciata
schiacciata con l'uva

25 g fresh yeast, 1 tablespoon dried active yeast or 1 sachet fast-action dried yeast

a pinch of sugar

250 ml warm water

500 g Italian '00' flour

2 egg yolks

2 tablespoons olive oil

½ teaspoon sea salt

175 g butter, softened

125 g demerara sugar, plus extra to sprinkle

finely grated zest of 1 unwaxed lemon

100 g walnuts, chopped

250 g black grapes, deseeded (Sangiovese wine grapes, if possible)

450 ml double cream or mascarpone

3 tablespoons icing sugar

100 ml Vin Santo

a Swiss roll tin, 23 x 32 cm, oiled

Serves 6

If you are using fresh yeast, mix it with the sugar in a medium bowl, then whisk in the warm water. Leave for 10 minutes until frothy. For other yeasts, follow the manufacturer's instructions.

Sift the flour into a large bowl and make a well in the centre. Pour in the yeast mixture, egg yolks, olive oil and salt. Mix until the dough comes together. Tip out onto a lightly floured work surface. Wash and dry your hands. Knead the dough for 10 minutes until smooth and elastic. It should be quite soft, but if it's too soft to handle, add more flour. Place in an oiled bowl, cover with clingfilm or a damp tea towel and leave to rise until doubled in size – about 1 hour.

To make the walnut butter, cream the butter and demerara sugar together then stir in the lemon zest and walnuts. Keep at room temperature.

Uncover the dough, punch out the air, then shape into a ball. Roll or pull the dough into a rectangle to line the prepared Swiss roll tin. Spread the walnut butter over the schiacciata base, add the grapes and sprinkle with demerara sugar. Cover with clingfilm or a damp tea towel and leave to rise for 1 hour until puffy and doubled in size.

Preheat the oven to 200°C (400°F) Gas 6. Uncover the dough and bake for 15 minutes. Turn the oven down to 180°C (350°F) Gas 4 and bake for 20 minutes, or until risen and golden. Cool slightly before turning out.

To make the Vin Santo cream, whisk the cream, icing sugar and Vin Santo together in a bowl until the mixture forms soft peaks. Cut the focaccia into wedges and serve with the Vin Santo cream.

This focaccia, enriched with egg and butter and infused with saffron, once symbolized wealth and generosity. The dough needs time to rise – the more sugar, butter and eggs in it, the longer it takes. I often let it rise slowly in the fridge overnight for the main rising, or even the final proving.

sweet Easter focaccia
focaccia di pasqua

25 g fresh yeast, 1 tablespoon dried active yeast or 2 teaspoons fast-action dried yeast

1 large pinch saffron threads or 2 small sachets powdered saffron

150 g sugar

200 ml hand-hot water

450 g Italian '00' flour

1 teaspoon salt

5 egg yolks

finely grated zest of 1 unwaxed orange and 1 unwaxed lemon

150 g unsalted butter, softened

1 egg, beaten

100 g whole blanched almonds

icing sugar, to dredge (optional)

a shallow cake tin, 25 cm, oiled

Makes 1 focaccia, 25 cm

Put the yeast and saffron into a large measuring jug and add a teaspoon of the sugar. Mix well, then pour in the hand-hot water and whisk until the yeast is dissolved. Leave in a warm place for 10 minutes until frothy.

Whisk 100 g of the flour into the yeast mixture to make a thick, smooth batter. Cover with clingfilm and leave to rise in a warm place for about 1 hour until doubled in size. (This could be done overnight in the fridge.)

Sift the remaining flour and salt into the bowl of a food mixer. Add the remaining sugar, egg yolks, orange and lemon zest, and beat until well mixed. Pour in the batter and beat until smooth and elastic – about 5 minutes. Cover the bowl with clingfilm and leave to rise in a warm place until doubled in size – about 2 hours.

Remove the clingfilm from the batter and gradually beat in the soft butter until shiny and elastic – another 5 minutes. The dough will be very soft. Tip out onto a lightly floured board and shape into a smooth ball. Transfer this to a sheet of baking parchment and roll out into a disc about 2.5 cm thick. Cover with an upturned bowl and leave to prove for 1 hour or until puffy. Alternatively, put the dough in the cake tin and leave to prove inside the tin.

Preheat the oven to 180°C (350°F) Gas 4.

Once the dough has risen, brush it lightly with the beaten egg, and lightly push the almonds randomly into the surface.

Bake for 1 hour until risen and golden. Serve dredged with icing sugar, if using, and with glasses of dessert wine.

pizzette and small bites

Goats' cheese has become as fashionable in Italy as it is here. The variety to use is the one with a snowy white rind that will hold its shape in the oven – just cut the pizza bases to fit the sliced cheese. Coupled with freshly made pesto, this is a marriage made in heaven. The pizzette are perfect served with drinks, as they can be assembled ahead of time and cooked at the last moment. If you make them beforehand, prick the bases all over to prevent them from rising too much, add the toppings, then cover and refrigerate until ready to cook.

goats' cheese and pesto pizzette
pizzette al caprino

½ recipe Basic Pizza Dough (page 12), making just 1 ball of dough

6 tablespoons Classic Pesto Genovese (page 19)

small goats' cheese log with rind (300 g)

4 fat garlic cloves, thinly sliced

extra virgin olive oil, to glaze

sea salt and freshly ground black pepper

a round biscuit cutter, 7 cm (optional)

Makes 12 pizzette

Preheat the oven to 220°C (425°F) Gas 7.

Uncover the dough, punch out the air and roll or pull very thinly on a well-floured surface. Using an upturned glass or a biscuit cutter, stamp out twelve 7-cm circles and lay on a lightly oiled baking sheet. Alternatively, cut the circles of dough to match the size of your goats' cheese log. Spread the pizzette with a little pesto.

Slice the goats' cheese into 12 slices and lay a slice on top of the pesto. Arrange a couple of slices of garlic on the goats' cheese and brush with olive oil. Season and bake for 8–10 minutes or until the cheese is beginning to melt. Serve immediately.

This amazingly savoury Ligurian focaccia is topped with a concentrated sauce of tomatoes, salted anchovies or salted sardines (hence the name), and whole melting cloves of garlic. It is perfect for outdoor eating, served in thin slices with a cold glass of wine or beer.

sardenaira

25 g fresh yeast, 1 tablespoon dried active baking yeast or 2 teaspoons fast-action dried yeast

½ teaspoon sugar

150 ml warm milk

500 g Italian '00' flour

7 tablespoons extra virgin olive oil

100 ml hand-hot water

2 onions, thinly sliced

1 kg fresh, very ripe tomatoes, peeled and chopped, or 1 kg (drained weight) tinned whole tomatoes

100 g anchovies or sardines in salt

12 or more whole garlic cloves, unpeeled

100 g or more small stoned black Ligurian olives

1 tablespoon dried oregano

sea salt and freshly ground black pepper

a rectangular baking tin, 28 x 43 cm and approximately 2.5 cm deep, oiled

Serves 10

In a large bowl, cream the fresh yeast with the sugar and whisk in the warm milk. Leave for 10 minutes until frothy. For other yeasts, follow the manufacturer's instructions.

Sift the flour with 1 teaspoon salt into a large bowl and make a well in the centre. Pour in the yeast mixture, 4 tablespoons of the olive oil and the hand-hot water. Mix together with a round-bladed knife, then use your hands until the dough comes together. Tip out onto a lightly floured surface, wash and dry your hands, then knead briskly for 10–15 minutes until smooth, shiny and elastic. Try not to add any extra flour at this stage – a wetter dough is better. If you feel the dough is sticky, flour your hands and not the dough. The dough should be quite soft. If it is *really* too soft to handle, knead in a little more flour.

To test if the dough is ready, roll it into a fat sausage, take each end in either hand, lift the dough up and pull and stretch the dough outwards, gently wiggling it up and down – it should stretch out quite easily. If it doesn't, it needs more kneading. Shape into a neat ball. Put it in an oiled bowl, cover with clingfilm or a damp tea towel and leave to rise in a warm, draught-free place until doubled in size – about 1½ hours.

Heat the remaining olive oil in a large saucepan, add the onions and cook for about 10 minutes until beginning to soften and colour slightly. Add the tomatoes and cook gently until collapsed and very thick. Meanwhile, split the anchovies, remove the backbone, rinse and roughly chop. Stir into the sauce and season to taste.

Preheat the oven to 180°C (350°F) Gas 4. Knock back the dough, knead lightly, then stretch and pat it out into the prepared tin, pushing the dough well up the edges. Spread the sauce on top of the dough, cover with the whole garlic cloves and the olives, then sprinkle with the oregano. Drizzle with a little olive oil and bake for about 1 hour until the pastry is golden. Serve sliced – hot, warm or cold.

These crisp little circles of fried pizza dough topped with a blob of tomato sauce, cool white mozzarella and fresh basil, are often served in bars with your *aperitivi*. Although best served straight from the pan, you can make the puffy pizza bases beforehand, let them cool and store in an airtight container. To reheat, put them in a preheated oven at 180°C (350°F) Gas 4 for 2–3 minutes, then add the toppings and serve. A wok makes a perfect fryer for these.

little fried Neapolitan pizzas
pizzelle aperte

½ recipe Basic Pizza Dough (page 12), making just 1 ball of dough

½ recipe Pizzaiola Sauce (page 17)

1 buffalo mozzarella, squeezed of excess water, then cut into tiny sticks

12 fresh basil leaves

vegetable or olive oil, for deep-frying

a round biscuit cutter, 5 cm (optional)

a wok or deep fat fryer

Makes about 12 pizzas

Uncover the dough, punch out the air and roll or pull very thinly on a well-floured surface. Using an upturned glass or a biscuit cutter, stamp out 12 or more 5-cm circles.

Heat the oil in a wok or deep fat fryer to 190°C (375°F) or until a tiny piece of dough sizzles instantly when dropped in. Fry the pizzas, 4 at a time, for 2–3 minutes or until puffed and golden. You will have to turn them now and again so that they colour evenly. Remove with a slotted spoon and drain on kitchen paper.

Top with a little pizzaiola sauce, a stick of mozzarella and a basil leaf. Serve immediately whilst still hot.

Almost like little muffins, these tiny treats hide a surprise when you bite into them – a tomato bathed in pesto and melting mozzarella. Make them in advance and reheat in a warm oven.

little stuffed focaccia muffins
focaccette ripiene

½ recipe Deep-pan Focaccia (page 86), making just 1 ball of dough, risen twice but uncooked

8 tablespoons Classic Pesto Genovese (page 19)

24 small cherry tomatoes

1 cow's milk mozzarella (*fior di latte*), squeezed of excess water, then diced

sprigs of thyme or rosemary, to decorate

rock salt

a round biscuit cutter, 7 cm (optional)

two 12-hole mini-muffin tins, oiled

Makes about 24 muffins

Preheat the oven to 200°C (400°F) Gas 6.

Uncover the dough, punch out the air and divide the dough into 4. Roll or pull each piece as thinly as you can on a well-floured work surface. Using an upturned glass or a biscuit cutter, stamp out 6 little circles. Place a scant teaspoon of pesto in the middle of each circle, add a little mozzarella, then top with a cherry tomato. Bring the sides up and over the tomato and pinch to seal.

Put the muffins, sealed-side down, in the prepared mini-muffin tins. Brush the tops with olive oil, push in a herb sprig and sprinkle with rock salt. Bake in the oven for 10–15 minutes until risen and cooked through. Tip out of the tins and eat warm, as a snack, with drinks.

Panzerotti or 'little fat bellies' from the Italian *pancia*, meaning 'tummy', are a great favourite in southern Italian pizzerias. The filling is usually some type of salami and cheese, and they can be quite large. They puff up like swollen bellies when deep-fried.

panzerotti

½ recipe Basic Pizza Dough (page 12), making just 1 ball of dough

100 g smoked mozzarella cheese, cut into small cubes

100 g *salame piccante* or chorizo, diced

200 g ricotta

60 g freshly grated Parmesan cheese

3 tablespoons chopped fresh basil

vegetable or olive oil, for deep-frying

sea salt and freshly ground black pepper

a round biscuit cutter, 8 cm (optional)

a wok or deep fat fryer

Makes about 15 panzerotti

Mix together the mozzarella, salami, ricotta, Parmesan and basil. Season.

Uncover the dough, punch out the air and roll or pull very thinly. Using an upturned glass or a biscuit cutter, stamp out about 15 little circles.

Place large spoonfuls of the filling onto one half of each pastry circle. Fold the other half over, pinching well to seal, then neaten the edges with a fluted pastry cutter.

Heat the oil to 190°C (375°F) in the wok or deep fat fryer and deep-fry the panzerotti in batches until puffed, crisp and brown. Flip them over to cook both sides evenly. Drain on kitchen paper and season with salt. Serve immediately whilst still warm and gooey.

I bought a factory-produced version of this in Tuscany and it inspired me to bake my own. It's so easy to make that you quickly get into the rhythm of preparing it until it becomes second nature. Use any leftover dough that you might have.

crispy pizza sheets
pizza croccante

1 recipe Basic Pizza Dough (page 12) or any leftover dough

2 teaspoons dried rosemary (optional)

extra virgin olive oil, to glaze

rock salt

2 large, heavy baking sheets, lightly oiled

Makes about 6 large sheets

Preheat the oven to 230°C (450°F) Gas 8, or as hot as you can.

Uncover the dough, punch out the air and knead in the dried rosemary (if using). Divide the dough into 6 and roll or pull it directly onto the prepared baking sheets. Press it out with your fingers as large and flat as you can. The dough should be so thin you can almost see through it – and it doesn't have to be even. Brush it lightly with olive oil and scatter with rock salt. Bake for about 8 minutes until golden, lightly bubbled, dry and crisp. Shatter the sheets like poppadoms to serve.

We all know the paper packets containing a couple of breadsticks which many Italian restaurants serve, but these are a more sophisticated version and can be made using leftover pizza dough. Just knead in the black pepper or any other flavouring that takes your fancy.

peppered breadsticks
grissini pepato

½ recipe Basic Pizza Dough (page 12), making just 1 ball of dough

2 tablespoons cracked black pepper

2 tablespoons extra virgin olive oil

25 g butter, melted

Makes about 20 breadsticks

Make the pizza dough according to the recipe on page 12, adding the cracked pepper to the ingredients. Mix the olive oil and melted butter together. Before the first rising, roll or pull the dough into a thin rectangle, brush all over with the olive oil and butter mixture and roll up loosely like a Swiss roll. Flatten with the palm of your hand, then lift it onto a floured work surface, cover with clingfilm and leave to rise for 30 minutes.

Preheat the oven to 200°C (400°F) Gas 6.

Flatten the risen dough with your hand again to knock out the air then roll out to a thickness of 5 mm. Cut into long, thin strips and twist like barley sugar. Lay these onto a baking sheet and mist with water. Bake for 5 minutes, mist again, then bake for a further 10–15 minutes until golden and crisp. Keep an eye on them while they are baking as they can burn.

In Ligurian dialect, a *ciappa* is a thin, flat stone that has been used for baking flatbreads since the dawn of time. Nowadays these stones, made from a type of slate, are used to cook meat and fish at the table. A *ciappa* can also mean a slate roof tile, and has come to mean a thin, crisply baked savoury biscuit, reminiscent of the shape of these ancient Ligurian roof tiles. Children eat these as crispbreads for breakfast. To ring the changes, flavour them by adding dried rosemary or oregano to the flour.

'roof tiles'
ciappe

1 tablespoon sea salt
100 ml warm water
250 g Italian '00' flour
2 tablespoons extra virgin olive oil

2 large, heavy baking sheets

Makes about 10 tiles

Mix the salt with the warm water until dissolved. Sift the flour into a medium bowl and make a well in the centre. Pour in the salty water and olive oil. Mix well, then knead the dough lightly for a couple of minutes until it is smooth. The dough should be firmer than that of pizza. Wrap it in clingfilm and leave to rest for 15 minutes.

Heat the oven to 180°C (350°F) Gas 4.

Divide the dough into 8. Roll or pull the pieces into long ovals. Roll them as thinly as you can (a couple of millimetres) and keep the work surface well floured to prevent sticking. Alternatively you can use a pasta machine to roll them out if you are making a large quantity.

Lay the tiles on the baking sheets and prick all over with a fork with large tines. Make sure they are liberally peppered with holes. Bake in the oven for 15–20 minutes or until evenly pale golden and dried out. Leave to cool on a wire rack and store in an airtight container for up to 2 weeks.

Here's another quick snack made from leftover pizza dough, and often served in bars. All you need is some fresh Parmesan cheese and you've got a delicious appetite-whetter. Just don't eat too many!

Parmesan fritters
chizze

½ recipe Basic Pizza Dough (page 12) or Sicilian Pizza Dough (page 14), making just 1 ball of dough

8 tablespoons freshly grated Parmesan cheese, plus extra to dust

vegetable or olive oil, for deep-frying

a round biscuit cutter (optional)

a wok or deep fat fryer

Makes about 16 fritters

Uncover the dough, punch out the air and roll or pull as thinly as you can, flouring the surface well. Using an upturned glass or a biscuit cutter, stamp out as many circles as you can – you can make them any size. Place a little mound of Parmesan in the centre of each one and fold in half, pinching the edges together.

Heat the oil in the wok or deep fat fryer to 190°C (375°F). A piece of stale bread dropped in should sizzle and turn golden in a few seconds. Fry in batches until puffed and golden on both sides. Drain well on kitchen paper, then toss the fritters in some grated Parmesan. Serve hot.

These *coccoli* ('little darlings'!) are a type of savoury doughnut or *bomboloni* flavoured with pancetta. I add lightly crushed fennel seeds, a flavouring that is very popular in Tuscany, especially with cured pork. They are deep-fried until crisp on the outside and soft inside and can be kept warm in the oven. Make sure they are piping hot and sprinkled liberally with sea salt when you serve them. Grind fennel seeds over them for a special finishing touch. These are especially wonderful if you have the chance to fry them in pure olive oil. The dough can also be rolled out thinly and cut into squares, then fried.

pancetta and fennel puffs
coccoli

200 ml milk

50 g pure lard, roughly chopped

40 g fresh yeast or 1 sachet fast-action dried yeast

400 g Italian '00' flour

50 g pancetta, finely diced

1 teaspoon fennel seeds, lightly crushed

vegetable or olive oil, for deep-frying

sea salt

a deep fat fryer

Makes 30–40 putts

Put the milk and lard in a saucepan and heat gently until the lard has melted. Don't let the milk get too hot. Crumble in the fresh yeast (if using) and whisk until dissolved. Sift the flour and a good pinch of salt into a bowl and make a well in the centre. If you are using fast-action dried yeast, stir it into the flour now. Pour in the warm milk mixture, and add the pancetta and fennel seeds. Mix to a soft dough, adding more flour, if necessary. Form into a ball, cover with clingfilm or a damp tea towel and leave to rise for 2 hours or until doubled in size.

Heat the oil in the deep fat fryer to 180°C (350°F). A piece of stale bread dropped in should sizzle and turn golden in a few seconds.

Uncover the dough, punch out the air and knead for 1 minute. Pull off small walnut-sized pieces of dough, about 2 cm, and roll into rough balls. Fry in batches for about 2–3 minutes until pale brown and puffy. Drain well and tip onto kitchen paper. Sprinkle with salt and serve whilst still hot.

websites and mail order sources

DEDICATED PIZZA SITES

www.pizzanapoletana.org
Italian site stating the specifications of true Neapolitan Pizza.

www.pizza.it
Italian/English site for all that is good about Italian pizza, with hints, tips and pizzeria guide.

www.correllconcepts.com/Encyclopizza
A wealth of information regarding making and baking pizzas, including dough and crust troubleshooting guide.

PIZZA OVENS

www.orchardovens.co.uk/domestic
Based in Preston, Lancashire, UK's sole importers and distributors of renowned Valoriani wood-burning ovens (for the garden or kitchen), handmade in Reggello, near Florence, Italy.

www.fornobravo.com
Friendly site for sale of outdoor and indoor pizza ovens, equipment and advice.

PIZZA ACCESSORIES

www.pizzakit.co.uk
Professional online store for pizzerias and a fantastic source for the passionate pizza-maker – all the pans, pizza peels etc. you'll ever need.

www.thecookskitchen.com
Great website for bakeware, including a heavy cast-iron bakestone or girdle, 27cm in diameter – ideal for piadines and scones, although not so good for oven pizzas.

www.silvernutmeg.com
Round and square bakestones, plus every kitchen tool you could need.

ITALIAN ONLINE FOOD SHOPS

Valvona & Crolla
19 Elm Row,
Edinburgh EH7 4AA
Telephone 0131 556 6066
www.valvonacrolla.com
Valvona & Crolla is Scotland's oldest delicatessen and Italian wine merchant, founded 1934. Their online shop sells their home-baked bread and an extensive range of cheeses, cookery books, coffee, kitchenware, pasta, rice, salami, sausages, oils, vinegars, whiskies and a fabulous Italian wine selection (they were voted Italian Specialist Wine Merchant of the Year 2005). They operate an efficient, speedy next-day delivery service to 90% of UK. They have a dedicated wine-tasting room and a demonstration theatre that seats 70 and is a venue in the yearly Edinburgh International Festival Fringe.

Carluccio's
29a Neal Street,
London WC2H 9QT
Telephone 020 7240 1487
www.carluccios.com
Owned by well-known Italian gastronome, Antonio Carluccio, this small Covent Garden delicatessen boasts an array of quality Italian produce such as rice and grains, cured meats, pasta, condiments, seasonal truffles, fruit and vegetables, chocolates and gifts. Branches now all over London.

Fratelli Camisa Ltd
53 Charlotte Street,
London W1V 3RG
Telephone 020 7255 1240
www.camisa.co.uk
Specialist in Italian, Spanish and Mediterranean foodstuffs, and a leading purveyor of Napoli/Milano salamis, Parma ham, cheeses, flour and much, much more.

www.esperya.com
This online mail-order company selects genuine, high-quality food products from all the different regions of Italy (olive oil, wines, honey, pasta, risotto rice, desserts, cured meats, cheeses, preserves, seafood).

www.savoria.co.uk
Savoria is a mail-order company that sells 'i veri sapori d'Italia' – the true tastes of Italy. Here you will find food created by Italian artisan producers, bringing hidden gems from all regions of Italy, including the islands, direct to your doorstep.

www.ItalianFoodDirect.com
Based in Northern Italy, this company will ship Italian speciality food worldwide (especially good selection of cheeses).

www.nifeislife.com
An online Italian supermarket stocking all the native Italian products, as well as cubes of fresh yeast, pizza-grade flour, olives, anchovies, capers, mozzarella, smoked provola etc.

ITALIAN FOOD SHOPS

Tavola
155 Westbourne Grove,
London W11 2RS
Telephone 020 7229 0571
*Italian deli owned by renowned chef Alistair Little –
they sell great home-baked focaccia slabs by
weight.*

I. Camisa and Sons
61 Old Compton Street,
London W1D 6HS
Telephone 020 7437 7610

Lina Stores
18 Brewer Street,
London W1R 3FS
Telephone 020 7437 6482

Gazzano & Son
167 Farringdon Road,
London ECIR 3AL
Telephone 020 7837 1586

Luigi's
349 Fulham Road,
London SW10 9TW
Telephone 020 7352 7739

Mortimer and Bennett
33 Turnham Green Terrace,
London W4 1RG
Telephone 020 8995 4145
*Fantastic little deli packed with many Italian
specialities.*

CHEESE

La Fromagerie
30 Highbury Park,
London N5 2AA
Telephone 020 7359 7440

2–4 Moxon Street
London W1U 4EW
Telephone 020 7935 0341

OLIVES AND OLIVE OIL

The Oil Merchant Ltd
47 Ashchurch Grove,
London W12 9BU
Telephone 020 8740 1335
*First port of call for olive oil and dressings, oils,
sauces, pasta, vinegars – what a choice!*

www.olivesdirect.co.uk
*Olives Direct has a selection of the finest quality
fresh olives available in the UK today. Nearly 30
types of quality fresh olives online.*

SPICES
The Spice Shop
1 Blenheim Crescent,
London W11 2EE
Telephone 0207 221 4448
www.thespiceshoponline.com
Dried herbs, spices, blends, grains, nuts and fruits.

HERB PLANTS AND SEEDS

Jekka's Herb Farm
Rose Cottage,
Shellards Lane, Alveston,
Bristol BS35 3SY
Telephone 01454 418 878
www.jekkasherbfarm.com
Suppliers of organic herb plants and seeds.

Laurel Farm Herbs
Main Road, Kelsale,
Saxmundham,
Suffolk IP17 2RG
Telephone 01728 668 223

www.theherbfarm.co.uk
*Marvellous selection of live herb plants delivered
to your door, including numerous varieties of
oregano and rosemary.*

www.seedsofitaly.com
*Real Italian seeds supplied mail-order for growing
your own Italian fruit, vegetables and herbs.
5 types of basil and over 20 varieties of tomato.*

USEFUL INFORMATION

www.slowfood.com
*Founded by Carlo Petrini in Italy in 1986, Slow
Food is an international association that promotes
food and wine culture, but also defends food and
agricultural biodiversity worldwide. It opposes the
standardization of taste, defends the need for
consumer information, protects cultural identities
tied to food and gastronomic traditions,
safeguards foods and cultivation and processing
techniques inherited from tradition and defends
domestic and indigenous animal and vegetable
species.*

www.gamberorosso.it
*Fascinating Italian gastronomic website with
information on books, food and wine, etc.*

www.wine-searcher.com
*Helps to find local importers of Italian wines, both
in the UK and the US.*

www.italianwinereview.com
*Interesting and impartial news and information
about Italian wines.*

www.italianmade.com
*The US official site for the foods and wines of Italy
– very interesting site to visit. Includes how to eat
Italian-style, where to eat and buy Italian produce
in the USA, history and lore of Italian foods and
wines.*

www.menu2menu.com/italglossary.html
*Helpful glossary of Italian menu and cooking
terms.*

index